SOUL SIDE OUT

Universal Laws to Healing and Living Your Best Life

SUMMER BOZOHORA

Printed in the United States of America

Library of Congress Control Number: 2020902945
ISBN: Softcover   978-1-64376-832-8
         eBook   978-1-64376-831-1
         Hardback   978-1-64376-833-5

Republished by: PageTurner, Press and Media LLC
Publication Date: 03/09/2020

To order copies of this book, contact:
PageTurner, Press and Media
Phone: 1-888-447-9651
order@pageturner.us
www.pageturner.us

Chapter Summary

INside-OWT
Immerse Audio GIFT Recording

Immerse
yourself in your inner being

Notice
what comes up

Own
what is presented

Willingness
to play and accept the metaphorical processes

Trust
that you are safe & guided

Go to: www.body-mind-soul-coaching.com/
immersion-audio-gift.html

To download your FREE Audio of how to get started
and Immerse into your inner being.

Dedications & Acknowledgements

I would like to express my gratitude to Saint Stephen's College instructors and its pedagogy for being the gem in the rough of our society that allowed my healing and any of this book to be possible. Thank you, particularly, to my instructor Marjorie Laplante and Lorraine Nicely – the matriarchs that forged the way for the rest of us.

To my mother, who was always ever so generous and her financial support and her unconditional generosity.

To my daughter, one of my greatest teachers. A wise being beyond her now 14 years. She lives and breathed this book everyday. I am beyond grateful for her presence and wisdom.

To my dear friend Jean Mitchell, for knowing me since I began my own soul journey, for being the editor of my masters thesis – which is the foundation of this book.

To Linda Verde, my book editor who was more than an editor, she is a coach and a co-creator. A person who strengthened my message through guidance and clarity. And to Petra Remy who gently nudged me to hire Linda and who played devil's advocate while reading the initial format of my book.

To Jessie Carriere, my accountability partner – who holds me, through relationship, to match my words with my intention and my soul's purpose. Mahsi Cho.

To my friends, Laura Graham and David Whalen, who invested in my gifts and gave very practical and uplifting advice.

To my friend and physician, Dr. Deborah Andrews, for the wisdom and unconditional support given to my growth, healing and in the writing of this book.

To DeeAnne Riendeau, the visionary who never gives up, encourages, mentors and creates. For the conventions, speaking opportunities and collaborative events that bring about the evolution of the healer's soul.

For my friends, Winnie Lau, RoseAnne Janzen, and Christiane Panesar. The world is forever enriched by the unique ways you show up in the world and, in particular, in my world and in my heart.

For Dr. Neil Tran and Silvia Schefzik, and the kindness and open-hearted way you received me and encouraged my own intuitive gifts and healing capacities as a collaborative colleague at the West Edmonton Naturopathic Wellness Centre.

For the Soul-Searchers, I have met so many beautiful souls that have crossed my path that have graced me with the trust to witness their transformations. It is the magic I live for.

Much gratitude goes to the healers and co-contributing authors that emerged in the process of writing this book: Olivia Kachman, Michelle Enns, Jillian Sodero, and Peggy Voth. For your co-creative soulful exploration and playful banter that evolved the content of this book. For your vulnerability and clear articulation of the soul and the healing possibilities much of our world has yet to discover.

Finally, I would like to thank Universal Matrix, that my Soul belongs to, for the direction I receive each day, in the most magical way, through Divine Guidance. I have been opened. I am open. I am ready to live and share this message. I accept.

Preface

Soul-Side Out

Learning to live your life soul-side out, in other words, learning to listen and be guided by your soul to live a healthy, joyful and meaningful life, is a natural process. Re-learning this process can be done in five steps and can be easily be remembered by the acronym IN-OWT or INside-OWT. (The acronym is defined more thoroughly in Chapter 6.)

INside-OWT is a way to be most present, a way to transcend the time-space reality and become a conduit to experiencing the Wave Function – the aspect of our mind that identifies with one-ness, unity and unconditional love – the part that transforms and heals. The process of healing from the inside-out guides one to becoming a witness or observer to your own, your client's, or loved one's truth or energy field in a very open, fluid and creative way.

The five-step process of INside-OWT is based in ten universal laws. These laws are defined and concretely laid out through the process and principles described in this book. It is not a process I created, but one I observe as inherent to life. I simply put words to it, as instructed and guided intuitively. The universal laws are reflected in the ideas and principles of quantum science and I have written this book with the goal of bridging the ideas of science and spiritual understanding in a simple new language.

I speak purely from my personal experience in life. My educational background includes psychology, counselling and art therapy, some medicine and alternative health therapies, even, by some luck, optical and optometric understandings. I chose not to enter into any of these specific fields for fear of being boxed in, in a way my soul could not bear. None of the professions or their codes of ethics, were close enough to resonate with what I believe the Universe/God's intended laws for true healing are.

What I am, is a renegade artist, thought leader, spiritual teacher and intuitive healer. I believe that the evolution of human consciousness is advanced through the unseen webs of soul-based information or what Carl Jung would have described as the Collective Unconscious. My expertise is other than traditional and I share my personal experience so those who find meaningful passages within this book can use it for their own personal healing.

When reading about my experience and my opinions, I ask that you, the reader, also claim for yourself the power of your own authority. Please take only that which resonates within yourself as true such that it helps you to understand your own life's experiences and live an authentic life.

*Note: Throughout this book, I have little stopping points called ***Reflections**. There you find suggested questions for your consideration, the answers to which may lead to understanding your inner truths. For a more interactive and deeper learning experience with this book, pause and take time to journal your answers.*

SOUL
SIDE OUT

Universal Laws to Healing
and Living Your Best Life

CHAPTER 1

Breaking Down

My Healing Crisis

My break down, or what I call my healing crisis, or awakening, began for me in India, at the age of twenty-four. During my studies for my bachelor's degree in business, I applied to travel and work on an exchange program, something I had been hoping for since high school, but was not allowed to do. India was not a country of my choosing, but I believe India chose me. I don't know why or how I was matched with India, but it came down to either I could go, despite my reservations and anxiety, or I'd miss the opportunity to travel. So, I went.

Before I traveled to India, life in my rich, suburban community was about as flavourful as eating cardboard; stiff and tasteless. Yet, somehow people still chose to live there, drawn like those fooled by the flashy activity of a Las Vegas Café selling false promises.

My community was one of the wealthiest in North America. Through my teen years and into my early twenties, I lived on an acreage surrounded by large homes and mansions – many with private indoor pools. The small community high school housed 200 students. Teenage girls are cliquey by nature, often driven by a seeming sense of entitlement among some rich girls and playing on the natural state of insecurity the age brings. The air seemed thick and suffocating, filled with personal and group tension. As cliques work, my refusing to be a part of them, made me a target. I was taunted, teased, beaten up at school, and even had the tires of my car slashed.

Our community could have had a reality show or soap opera created from its dramatic nature. There was a higher than average number of deaths and suicides. One distinct memory is of a neighbour, a plastic surgeon. When I was 16, my family was invited over for appetizers and to share a drink or two… or three… We toured his large home and were led to the balcony to share appetizers and conversation. I remember him telling me how he could fix the dimple on the bottom of my nose. I wasn't even aware of it until he suggested he could 'fix it' as if it was an unsightly and abhorrent flaw on my face. I was taken aback, finding his comment extremely shallow. Based on his personal viewpoint of beauty, perhaps he thought me a potential client with wealthy parents who would see the value of such superficial surgery.

At that moment, I was quiet. I said absolutely nothing because I was stunned and didn't know what to say. My look and my silence spoke for me. I was aghast and my quiet rejection of the offer for services changed the feeling tone of our exchange.

This conversation with me began in his role as a successful plastic surgeon with a lucrative career and something to offer me. My quiet rejection left a need for him to pursue a different avenue if he were to connect with or impress me. Some people, those immersed in the outside markers of success in their lives, wouldn't care about my young perspective. But, that was not the case with him. In that moment, I felt he respected me and, at the same time, had an undeniable and desperate need for my approval, which left me feeling a strong sense of of aversion and disgust toward him.

The energy of that exchange was very strong, and at the age of 16 I didn't know what he was seeking from me. Looking back, it seems that my strong sense of self worth, my unshakable belief that my dimple was absolutely fine with me, triggered an emptiness within him.

What happened the next day was shocking. He killed himself and was found in a room of his house. That this tragedy happened soon after I felt his desperate need for my approval has never left my mind. Because of the feeling tone I sensed from him on the day of our exchange, his suicide made sense to me. Being sixteen, I could not put into words what I felt before the tragedy occurred. Years later, I understand that outside appearances masked an inner turmoil of meaninglessness. From the outside looking in at the conversation, he looked proud of his home and confident and self-assured speaking about plastic surgery, his field of expertise, yet a day later he left it all behind.

Aside from acknowledging that he had died, my parents never discussed it with me. Nothing was ever said about anyone's perceptions, ever. That would be far too uncomfortable a conversation. I have forgotten about this experience for different lengths of time, but the energetic impression was stamped into my understanding of life and my knowing.

On the outside the members of the rural community I lived in seemed wealthy. On the inside its inhabitants were often suffering and depraved.

> "There are many in the world who are dying for a piece of bread. . . . The poverty in the West is a different kind of poverty – it is not only a poverty of loneliness but also of spirituality. There's a hunger for love, as there is a hunger for God." Mother Theresa (Fox, 1991)

This "rich" culture was my 'normal'. And although I often had a feeling something was missing in my life, I only knew this way of life.

> "The ways our culture shapes us are so integral to our lives that how we think seems perfectly natural . . . So deeply embedded in our lives are the ways of our culture that changing them is often difficult." (Fancher, 1995, p. 29)

Had I not travelled to India and been subjected to the immense cultural discordance, from a familial but also societal perspective, I would never have written this book. I could not possibly have understood all the layers of reality that were unveiled to me without un-embedding myself from my own culture. India's aromas – fresh herbs and spices, garbage and flowers – and the bright colours of silks, awakened my senses. The deeply ornate temples of prayer and carefully constructed altars piqued my curiosity. As a child of an atheist and an agnostic, there was no mention of God or Spirit in our home, so the idea of prayer was new to me.

My Indian Family

My hosts – an Indian family of four – were gracious, poor and yet, particularly generous and kind. My Auntie and Uncle, (adults are referred to as this in India) who were of a similar age to my own parents, gave up their sleeping area for me. Although they were a couple, they chose to sleep on a single bed! I was aghast, but unwilling to challenge my adult hosts, being most unsure of the cultural protocols.

I was given the nicest and largest bed and the only wardrobe space they owned. They had few other possessions – only two kitchen chairs and a small table. They often sat on the floor in a room with no other furniture but their carefully constructed altar in a corner of the room.

Their unquestionable generosity left me baffled. I came from a wealthy country where many of my friends or their children would not share their bedroom, nor be so hospitable. Yet, here they put me in a private room and bathroom, and treated me, it seemed, as if I were royalty.

I was the only white person in the town and I rode to work, sitting in the women's section at the front of the bus. Despite there being standing room only and people being jam-packed like sardines, I had a seat to myself. I was left sitting alone. I startled one young girl terribly when she sauntered up to the seat beside me. She let out a scream when she laid her eyes on what must have looked very ugly and ghostly. At five or six years old, this young girl had never seen a foreigner before.

At my home in India, I observed rats climbing around our yard and up into the large garbage pile. No one paid any mind. I watched our maid – who came from a much lower caste than my hosts, washed my clothes by beating them against a large rock not far from the garbage pile. I could not believe my eyes.

My travels throughout India, brought me face-to-face with extreme poverty. I saw children with broken legs begging for money. I was told that parents would sometimes break their children's legs so the children could bring in more money. I never would have imagined the kind of desperation that would make a parent do such a thing. It was a brutal reminder that I came from a very different background. The discordance I felt between India's culture and my own initiated a flow of awareness I could not contain. I had no distractions: no T.V., no telephone, no friends (except my Indian family), nor access to any substances that might help me deny or avoid the onslaught of suppressed memories.

Unconscious beliefs, perceptions and childhood traumas began to bubble up to the surface of my consciousness. I began to read, reflect and journal for the first time in my life. I began to enjoy my time alone and the flow of awareness was both challenging and refreshing. While this new awareness was rising within me, I got a call from home that my parents had chosen to get a divorce and were separating. Hearing that news shocked me, but I was ready to go home.

Plane Ride Back to Canada

During the 24-hour flight home from India, my childhood eczema flared up, covering my body. As I sat in the plane, anxiously anticipating my arrival home, I vigorously scratched my elbow folds. The skin was fragile and it was soooo itchy. I scratched my arms to the point of bleeding, and within a day, one of the openings in my skin developed a large boil the size of a golf-ball and just as hard.

At the time, I was unaware of the emotional upheaval surging up from the depths of my soul and unaware that my physical symptoms had any relationship to anything but the surface of my skin. I was given a series of tests by infectious disease specialists at the hospital to determine the cause of the infection and the boils. They told me they

SOUL-SIDE OUT: UNIVERSAL LAWS TO HEALING AND LIVING YOUR BEST LIFE

had no real explanation for it. My immune system seemed normal and they told me I would likely just have to keep taking antibiotics and have this issue for the rest of my life! ... I was stunned! These *specialists* could not help me!

I was given several prescriptions for antibiotics to rid me of the boils and streptococci blood infection causing them. When I took the antibiotics, the boil on the surface of my skin receded, only to be followed by another as soon as I finished taking the medicine.

Within our healthcare system, the solutions for what ails us is often some form of drug. There is not much else, at least not in conventional medicine. The idea is to fight or kill whatever invades our body. In Chapter 3, I will talk about this very interesting, fear-based paradigm for treating illness and disease.

After several new boils and rounds of antibiotics, I began searching for information to explain what was going on in my body. Although I don't remember the book or where I located the passage that shifted my awareness, I do remember that boils and the green puss that oozed from them represented *long-held, repressed anger erupting through the surface.* Aha! That's it! My whole body responded with an undeniable, YES! The feeling was so strong, I knew it was confirming a truth within me.

I had been holding anger and confusion in my body for years. It was finding its way out as I journaled, dreamed, sketched out and scribbled my body sensations, emotions, memories, and images. I began to trust my body and what it was telling me. I refused the last antibiotics prescribed for me and haven't had a boil since. The healing went deeper. I stopped having issues with eczema all together, and it had been a lifetime chronic issue.

As I began healing myself, my body, my distorted beliefs and emotional traumas, I was called to work with others. I began counselling training and volunteering at the 24-hour crisis centre. On the 24- hour crisis line, I came to understand more about human crisis, peoples' fragility and the scope of our human suffering.

* *Reflection Break*

Q1 Have you ever had a symptom or body pain, that spontaneously changed or resolved without medical attention? If so, recall what it was and what was going on in your life at the time.

CHAPTER 2

Breaking Open – Navigating Yourself to Greater Health

Your Health Provider's Perspective

In my own life struggles, emotional and physical, I learned one of the most important aspects of healing is choosing the right person to help you navigate through your experience to greater health. How well we recover, grow or heal depends on knowing what we need and matching that to the person from whom we seek guidance.

It is important to understand the care-provider's perspective because there are many different models, theories and approaches to health care. Being aware of this wide menu of views about health when choosing who and how they may help us, is vital in preventing harm.

Personally, I first sought help by consulting a psychologist. There wasn't a lot of thought behind my decision, I just wanted help navigating a very confusing part of my life. As I began to make sense of my suppressed anger, memories and confusion, I found myself lost in an identity crisis. During this time, I was unable to relate naturally to people, felt very insecure and often overwhelmed with emotion and fear.

During my life, I may have been able to be labeled with one diagnosis or another, or been prescribed drugs, but I had not. And because I had not, the psychologist I chose questioned the validity of my life history. She was unable to understand how I could have gotten through my family history and childhood sexual abuse without using drugs. She never asked me how I did cope. Instead, the psychologist dismissed my experience of child sexual abuse as false. I was shocked, disgusted and grateful that my internal compass was strong enough to keep me from collapsing under her care.

My truth was questioned because I had not taken drugs that a mental health professional believed necessary in cases of trauma and abuse. She practised from this perspective and because I did not fit what she believed to be true, she invalidated my experience. This was not helpful for my healing, but it did make me aware of what I didn't want as I searched other solutions to maintain my sanity.

* Reflection Break

Q1 What kind of care have you sought?

Q2 Was it helpful ? –did it help you process the meaning of your symptoms at a deep level? Or did it skim the surface?

Q3 Or was the care you received harmful in some way?

My primary way of coping was to dive into my inner world. I explored my newly discovered world and found it rich and meaningful. Imagery, art and journaling – the type one might call spirit speak or automatic writing – oozed effortlessly out of me, healing me on the way.

Through my personal healing experience, I was drawn to re-enroll in University. This time I entered a visual arts program preparing for a degree in Art Therapy. Artistic expression, colour, my dreams and my journals saved me. They gave me a place to go to gain insight and piece together my fractured self. My memories before the age of five had been a complete blank, but the pages of my journals begin to fill with them. Through my dreams and artwork, memories and body sensations began to surface, so did my energetic and intuitive awareness. I became aware of being sexually abused as a child. At a young age I was molested. Fortunately for me, it was not a repeated occurrence.

I saw the perpetrator by chance several years later. I was travelling on a summer vacation with my family and ended up stopping for a swim in an outdoor pool. This person owned the pool. Although I was unable to verbally express my feelings or consciously remember the circumstances that created the rage I felt toward this person, my body's emotional-energetic relay system chose a very clear message. I deliberately shat in the swimming pool with a sense of great satisfaction.

While the little brown floaters I created bobbed around in the pool, I pretended I had no idea how they got there. I was older than the other children in the pool so I knew I was less likely to be suspected as the culprit. Pooping in the pool was the only way I could safely communicate my feelings. Looking back, I see it was a clever way to mirror the secrecy of the perpetrator's behaviour toward me.

The catch-all term for many of these events in our lives is *trauma*. Many of us have these types of distorted, twisted energetic histories embedded on a cellular level within our bodies. The energetic threads go back generations and generations, enduring through the ages of our ancestors, through world wars and bombings, violence and unspeakable abuses. As subtle or hidden the effects may seem to be, we are affected. These things may be hidden from open speech and our daily activities, but the effects of past events matter. Many human experiences are energetically wreaking havoc within our bodies, minds and souls, festering in the unconscious collective of our human psyche.

I have had my share of dramatic life experiences. War, addictions, abuses and atrocities are extreme, but any kind of untruth, secret, or hiding, is a distortion of truth and disconnects us from our inner knowing. As babies, and children, we are spongy, absorbent energetic beings. It is easy to absorb the anger, confusion, depression, and worthlessness of others as if it were our own. Doing this for prolonged periods of time, without any tools with which to circumvent the effects, distorts our perceptions and feelings about the world and ourselves.

Many symptoms, illnesses, diseases and visual blurs are often really clever ways to mirror a sense of internal distortion and disconnection from the Universe/Creator/Higher Purpose/God.

The Symptom Imperative

Dr. John E. Sarno, has created a term I think is very important for people to know. The term is **Symptom Imperative.** The *Symptom Imperative* operates within a series of disorders that fall within an area of study and are referred to as psychosomatic medicine. In his books, *The Divided Mind* and *The Epidemic of Mind-Body Disorders*, Dr. Sarno describes psychosomatic disorders as falling into two categories:

1. Those disorders that are directly induced by unconscious emotions such as pain problems (including, but not limited to back pain and migraine headaches) and common gastrointestinal conditions including reflux, ulcers, irritable bowel syndrome, skin disorders such as eczema, allergies and many others.

2. Diseases in which unconscious emotions play a role, *but are not the only factor,* include autoimmune disorders, cardiovascular conditions, and cancer (Sarno, 2007, 1997).

To these two categories, specified by Dr. Sarno, I would add a third, vision problems – the need for glasses, blurred vision, strabismus and amblyopia (lazy eye). Degenerative eye diseases and inflammatory conditions influenced by autoimmune disorders are also affected by unconscious emotions or *what we don't want to see.*

The purpose of the **symptom imperative** is to distract the conscious mind, from what we have been taught are unacceptable or undesirable feelings or expressions. The type of symptom and its location in the body is not important so long as it fulfills its purpose of diverting attention from what is transpiring in the unconscious.

Every condition in our lives exists because there is a need for it in one way or another, either on the time-space level or on the soul level. ... A specific sickness is the natural physical outcome of specific thought patterns and/or emotional disharmonies. Illnesses, ailments, disorders, and diseases represent the **final warning system.** They are coded messages from the body to the effect of what is happening and what needs to happen. In effect, then, illnesses and ailments teach us, expand us, and move us on (Khalsa, 1991).

Illness and even injuries do not start with physical symptoms, they begin long before the physical symptoms show up. At times, it can start energetically even before we are born, within the energetic field of our family into which we are born. These illnesses, symptoms, etc., may not even be about our energy, thoughts or emotions in this life. The symptoms may emerge as part of an energetic pattern that has been pre-established through the genetic field and perpetuated through the unchanged emotional and psychological reactions of the parents and societies – who unconsciously perpetuate certain patterns in their children and in their citizens.

We belong. We belong to a matrix of human consciousness. To believe, act and treat conditions as if the context and culture with which these conditions arise are not part of a condition's manifestation, is a form of blindness or insanity. Dr. Sarno calls this lack of awareness – the not including unconscious emotions as potential risk factors in these types of disorders – criminal.

In our culture, it is far more acceptable to talk about and address physical pain than it is emotional pain. This starts when we are children. As human beings, we have a universal desire for connection and to be deeply nurtured by our parents, or someone within the community to which we were born. We need to know that others care and that we have an effect on our world based on our existence. If we cannot get the sense that we belong and are important emotionally, often the next best way to get attention is through physical symptoms or pain.

In the context of our historically emotionally repressed culture, parents are more able to respond to physical pain or symptoms. It's easier to attend to children when their pain is physical and visible. Physical symptoms can be attended to without disturbing or awakening the parents' repressed feelings or unresolved traumas and children can get the attention they crave. Unfortunately, restraining our deepest held emotional and spiritual yearnings for life and hiding them through physical symptoms distorts our life energy and has long-term consequences.

No matter how we attempt to separate the mind and body, or try to placate the body's symptoms, our attempts eventually stop working. The collapse of this mechanism most often occurs under stress or pressure and results in a migraine headache, emotional or nervous breakdown, burn-out, accident or injury, or life or health crisis.

Often, under these circumstances, defences can drop and the mind can no longer be tricked into believing the emotions are not there. The energy of the psyche and the soul can no longer be physically repressed. Because the body is like a diverter or relay system meant as a divine channel of communication between our soul and our physical reality, it's only a matter of time before symptoms appear that begin to call us toward a more integrated mind-body experience of life.

This is because, as human beings, whether we are aware of it or not, we are constantly asking questions about life and death – its meaning and purpose. And, there is nothing that calls life's meaning and purpose into question as much as personal crisis or illness, because they strike to the core of what we believe about life.

The Paradigm of Self-Healing

Once, I presented an introductory self-healing collegium to my peers – theology students. Many of them were chaplains, ministers, nurses, and counsellors. One of them asked the most important question that arises when people consider what self-healing means, "What do you say to a client who is dying, whose peers, church, and family members tell them that they aren't praying hard enough?" She continued, "If they are told they can self-heal, won't they blame themselves for their experiences, disease, or illness?"

My answer was yes – often people do accept blame; however, blame is a concept that arises within a particular belief system. Blame, judgment and punishment co-exist within a belief system that sees God or Creator as outside of oneself and more powerful than oneself. It views God as punishing and to be feared.

This type of relationship with Source makes us feel helpless, insignificant and fearful. Thus, if a client accepts blame for their state of health, they inevitably believe that something about themselves is wrong or bad. As a result one prays harder, begs and pleads because we believe ourselves powerless.

What if the Universe supports you? What if you are safe, no matter what? What if your energy is an integral part of the Universe? Why, then, are you experiencing your symptoms or life situation? Is there a deeper, richer meaning besides the idea that your symptoms or some part of you is wrong or undeserving?

Self-healing presumes the essential strength, wisdom and integrity of people who live a life in service to Source. Many spiritual traditions of the world know this inner resilience and call it by many names: Inner light, Essential Essence, Still-point, Soul, and Holy Spirit to name a few. Finally, life and health includes death. Death is a completion, not a punishment.

We all die, it just depends on why, how and when. Many would find it ideal to die of natural causes, feeling ready to transition and leave our bodies after a long, good life. Most of us probably would like to die without pain, with peace in our hearts, and at a time we feel we have come to completion with our chosen life path and goals. Our fear of death often has more to do with not feeling at peace with our why, how and when. We get so busy doing other things and focussing on external goals, distractions or pursuits that we can be surprised when what appears to be a sudden health condition sneaks up on us.

If we are aligned with our soul during life, we will also be at peace with death. During our lifetime, if we believe our soul is innately radiant, when we sink into our quiet inner realm we are filled with peace. If, however, we fear our inner world because it may show us our brokenness, flaws and failures, we avoid it.

A common fear of stopping our busy lives and listening to our inner realm is because of what we believe we will find there. If we believe we are not good or whole inside, we may be reluctant to stop and rest, afraid we will find a lurking emptiness, a terrible aching void that nothing can fill. This wide-open inner space, can feel like an abyss that is in opposition to all that is visible and safe, so we may choose to remain in the realm of form, with things we can see and touch and that we perceive are subject to our control. So, we quickly fill all the blanks on our calendar with tasks, accomplishments, and errands to fill the time and space.

The story of my plastic surgeon neighbour is not unusual. Many people lead lives, working and believing they need to continue in soul-sucking positions or relationships that slowly wear them down until they realize they are unhappy and sick.

With my clients if, for but a moment, I see this fear, it excites me because I know what is around the corner. They have found the creative void of emptiness, which is richly fertile with potential. When this happens, it is as if they enter a field of being – a universal creative process in which willing explorers are able to tame their inner demons regardless of how big, ferocious or deep their doubt, sorrow, fear or loss is.

The creation that happens within the stillness of our inner world does more than just allow one to bear life. Creation is unlimited, it is infinite in its possibilities and these same possibilities are intrinsic to each individual. When people embrace the principles of wholeness, it awakens a life-serving energy that motivates and sustains them.

Life events are guidance tools, not punishments and there are always signs and opportunities that allow you to find the answers you seek. It's just that sometimes we are creatures of habit or comfort. What we know often is more comfortable than change. In the following section, two women have written their stories, in their own words, of what it took to transform their illnesses and live from the soul-side out.

Addiction as a Soul-Sickness

Jill Sodero

I think in life there are opportunities called wake-up calls. They don't often feel like "opportunities" at the time. The biggest wake-up call for me was finally seeing through the haze, pain, denial, and loneliness to realize that I was in the throws of active addiction and all the hurt and suffering it causes. Not me! Wealthy housewife. Mother of three. Educated. Spiritual.

It wasn't until I had already committed to a healing path, and all the stuff that brings up, that I began to open up the energetic and emotional pain held in my body. Past trauma, false beliefs and fear drove my insane thinking, and the feeling that there was an emptiness deep within where my soul should be.

I grew up in a stable and loving home at first. The first trauma was the death of my brother when I was a young child. The memory of that day and the pain I experienced witnessing my parents' despair and seeing him away seared into my mental, physical and emotional body. I'm sure that was the beginning of what would, over 3 decades later, be identified as post traumatic stress disorder (PTSD) and generalized anxiety disorder.

In the interim, I just grew up thinking there was something wrong with me.

When I was in elementary school my father began drinking and using drugs and the violence, insanity, and lack of safety and stability began. I remember one night, as he rampaged through the house, shockwaves of pain surged down my arms and jarred in my hands. I felt the anger and hurt surging through my body and I clenched my fists. I'm sure it happened many times, but I recall that night – both the pain and the power. It felt like it was the only power I had. It felt like a defiance that was all mine, and I wanted to hold onto it. I was empowered by my anger, even if it meant turning it in on myself. Fifteen years later I was diagnosed with osteoarthritis in my hands, way too young for my age, and I'm sure that was related to that holding on to emotional and energetic pain I had experienced all those years before. It was still there, and was finally manifesting physically.

As systems go in families who face issues like mine did, everyone adopts a particular role. Mine was to fix things and to make sure everything was taken care of and under control. I felt insane. The problem was that I didn't realize the insanity was the situation, not me. A lot of what drove my addiction was emotional pain and growing up in a codependent alcoholic family and not having anyone who could help me understand my thoughts or support a healthier way for me to cope. I became proficient at separating from my body and the emotional effort and energy it required. I often couldn't even feel my body anymore, except for the pain. I sometimes still struggle with the physical aspect today. Back then, emotion rode in waves, and I was like an inexperienced surfer carried away on a surfboard. My thoughts ran wild, and I was out of control riding the waves. My body hurt with the shame, guilt, anger, fear and self-loathing.

I didn't know how to define all this at the time.

Drinking was a natural means of coping. It was the model I had grown up with, and it was the legacy passed down through generations in my family. I drank as much as possible in my teens and during university, but I thought I knew better than to fall into the trap of alcoholism. I was able to choose not to drink while I was pregnant or during the early years of my children's lives.

Then the day came when I decided I wanted to drink socially again. I made the decision, and I heard an inner voice say, without any judgment but as a truth and acknowledgment, that I would be an alcoholic. I even looked around when I heard the voice because it was so loud. Then I shrugged my shoulders and off I went! I think many of us have inner voices we often disregard – some may be inaudible or subtle, but I distinctly remember this one. Looking back, if the voice was that loud, maybe I could have had a conversation with that part of me – that inner voice. I didn't want to hear it, though. I didn't have time! I had things I wanted to do, goals to accomplish. My ego won out and I dampened that inner voice.

This began a decline over the years until I became very ill, although many people still didn't know. It's amazing how well it can be hidden. My marriage was, of course, affected, and I decided to take my husband to a counsellor because he needed fixing. My counsellor was a gift. Along with her counselling degrees and extensive experience in her field, she had a theology degree, spiritual gifts, and she recognized the soul connection in healing. She looked over her eyeglasses one day and asked me if perhaps next time I'd like to discuss my primary relationship (which was the alcohol). This comment hit something within me and took my breath away. That is when things began to change. She sparked my awareness of a problem I just couldn't ignore. The seed was planted, and my journey to healing began, before I even realized it had. It wasn't my husband who needed to be fixed. That part was none of my business. It was me – my wounded self that needed self-care, acknowledgment and new strategies.

I learned that it's okay to say I'm struggling. I finally became a tad willing and more honest with myself. These two seeds, willingness and honesty, would be what moved mountains for me. I had done some counselling before, but now I had to become vulnerable and open. It didn't come without resistance, but finally I was ready to see, and the

Universe unfolded easily with resources and opportunities for help and healing. It's a good thing I accepted them.

The support I received was not from the places I expected. It wasn't my mom or my husband. I had to challenge my childhood learning and beliefs, things like: you don't get help; psychologists are stupid; and, you absolutely do NOT take meds because it means you are weak. The message was that I needed to figure out my own stuff. It's my problem. It's my attitude and my fault.

Finally, I took a stand for my own needs and did what was right for me – no matter what others thought. I realized that I was dying, no one was getting it, and it was really serious.

I went away to a recovery centre for five weeks. I chose to step out of the life I knew, and back into me. It wasn't easy. I was scared people would find out and judge me, but somehow I was given the strength to do it anyway. This pivotal decision would be much further reaching than I ever could have imagined. It was the most self-honouring act of love I had ever done for myself, and the hardest one. All the pain, shame and confusion needed a voice, and I gave it to them. My inner little girl needed to be heard and to heal. Taking time for my addiction opened the doors to all the other underlying issues. This became the path to healing on all levels – a journey I continue today.

Addiction is known as a soul sickness. When asked how I would define soul, the first response is an emotional one. When one has felt they have lost their soul and the void is so great, the gift of retrieving it is the most profound joy. It has been a big part of my life to get to know my soul, and to embrace all of my humanness – even the undesirable parts. I knew my soul when I was a little girl. I know her again now. I think I came here to know my soul. One must know how it feels to be without it to deeply recognize what it feels like to find it.

For me, the soul is here-ness; all other things drop away. In my soulfulness there's no judgment that I'm not good enough or worthy enough. There's no fear. There's no elation either. There just is. It is not the same void I experienced in addiction. This void is a sense of being whole rather than fragmented. In my average day, when I feel connected with my soul, there's peace, acceptance and possibility. Emotions like grief and anger come, but only as experiences rather than states of being that I get caught up in. I feel connected and safe when I feel my soul. My ego is taking a time-out on the bench, and I can put my arm around it and we can laugh together at the crazy, ego shit we did today. How human!

Before my healing, and meeting my soul again, I never felt like I belonged. Not in my body. Not in this world. My thoughts and emotions were torrents and I was just trying to survive. This has invited me to go deep within, to the eye of the storm, and discover who and what I am. The greatest gift in my healing has been connection.

Today, I am recovered. I must keep a spiritual connection to stay well, and I have to be in contact with all parts of myself. My body is healthy, especially considering the amount of anxious energy it naturally holds, and the arthritis in my hands has progressed at a very slow rate. I usually don't even notice it's there.

I still tend to put myself last sometimes. It's more natural for me not to bother taking care of myself in the subtle, nurturing ways. My mind and body sometimes still feel detached. I know I'm detached when my mind gets too focused, I hold my breath, and my body tenses up. It's like my mind doesn't want to pause to attend to the rest of me. But when I sit and choose to feel my body, my mind reconnects with it.

During my life, my body has not felt like a priority. For most of my life it was like a dumping ground for unexpressed or unacceptable feelings. As I grew, what I noticed is that when significant adults in my life, such as teachers, mentors or family members, didn't acknowledge or respond appropriately when I would tell them something confusing, or violent happened, I felt an incredible amount of distrust and fear. I felt unsafe. So much fear arose in me and couldn't be vented. There was no place for the energy to move so it got sucked inward. For me, it was a powerful sense of anger and defiance that I carried and held in my body.

This type of anger turned inward toward oneself disconnects us from our true nature. I've found my spiritual and healing path to be quite pragmatic and practical. I have to show up, get conscious, and do things that keep me connected and in service. I've had to learn how to care for myself deeply, and not live my life to please others or to fulfill an idea I have of what I should be. I'm still a work in progress, of course, but working on myself and getting help doing it, is the best thing I've ever done. It hasn't been easy, but it has been worth it!

I often feel joy in the moment, even at unusual times like when I'm under a lot of stress. There is a tremendous faith in living that comes with having a joyous moment just because you're present to experience it. When I feel off, I know it will pass and I can do something useful to help someone in the meantime.

Through my lived experience, I believe I am being asked to form a relationship with every aspect of life and myself. I was in so much mental, emotional, physical and spiritual pain that I pursued an unconscious life through substance, shopping and people pleasing. I've had to choose a conscious life to get well. I begin to observe things, how I feel and think in response, and negative emotions and energy lose their power. The gift has been healing, and better mental, emotional and physical health.

When I get right down to it, I think the only thing that really matters is connection – to my authentic self and therefore also to the authentic nature of others. There's a sense of overwhelming love. Fear can be mixed in, as I still have it, but I get better at watching it all and knowing none of it defines me. I simply can observe the energy and let it go.

This has been a process of learning to live in the moment and gain connection and awareness. I see addiction and co-dependence as being out of alignment and not in true connection with oneself or others. I'm grateful to be learning to embrace the unknown, trust life, and appreciate every one of my experiences. I wouldn't be me without them, and I wouldn't change a thing about my journey. For me, this has become an immense feeling of purpose and a life well lived.

Soul Alignment: Essentials to my Healing

Michelle Enns

I have personally transformed my life and have overcome traumatic experiences by using various techniques of energy healing. It took me over 20 years of suffering before I turned to energy work as a way to heal. I write this now to raise awareness of how healing involves not just the physical but also the mental, emotional and spiritual components of a whole being.

I grew up in a dysfunctional family dealing with alcoholism, divorce, poverty, and a father who worked away. I remember being angry, disappointed, thought that life was unfair and blamed my parents for how I felt in life. An only child, I primarily felt lonely and alone. In order to succeed in school and University, I had to shut off my emotions and memories from my childhood and focus on my studies. I thought I'd put it behind me but never really even acknowledged the emotions I had.

As an adult I struggled with chronic migraines for over 20 years, infertility for eight years, grief and severe stress. I left work on a stress leave and was diagnosed with major depression and anxiety, which I lived with for over 15 years. I tried several types of medication and was forced to go to group therapy. During that time the only real awareness I noticed was that I was super angry at my father and expressed it a bit in some exercises. The depression and anxiety remained. My health continued to deteriorate. I saw medical doctors and had tonnes of tests that ruled out everything they knew of and by default they determined I had symptoms of both chronic fatigue syndrome and fibromyalgia. I was told there was nothing that could be done for it.

After a few years of that, I turned to a naturopathic doctor who discovered that I had chemical toxicity. There were plastics, insecticides, herbicides, air pollution (cigarettes and diesel had always bothered me), mercury, and lead in my blood. I began detoxifying and then a year later was diagnosed with breast cancer. I received vitamin injections and ozone therapy, which helped tremendously and I chose to have a mastectomy. A year later I still wasn't bouncing back like the naturopathic doctor had hoped and I started wondering if I should address the emotional issues of my past rather than only focussing on the physical symptoms. I asked my naturopathic doctor his opinion of how much he thought emotions contributed to health. He said, "at least 40%," and as I researched I found that some specialists say emotions and stress were 80% or more responsible for our health, illness, and physical symptoms. Dr. Bradley Nelson, who wrote *The Emotion Code*, and Dr. Darren Weissman, developer of *The LifeLine Technique*, have these things to say.

> "90% of all pain that we experience is due to trapped emotions, to emotional baggage . . . those emotions stay with us and cause our diseases and much of our self sabotage." (Nelson, 3013)

"The core of every symptom, stress and disease are emotions, memories and traumatic perceptions that are buried in our subconscious mind." (Weissman, 2013)

For me, cancer was a blessing and a wake-up call that prompted me to start taking control of my own life and healing. I researched, radically changed my diet, and learned that we need to detox physically and emotionally for optimal health.

The AMA (American Medical Association) says that "80% of all health issues are stress related." Dr. Joe Dispenza, a neuroscientist and author, says that,

"humans can turn on the stress response just by thought alone. Our thoughts create our emotions, which create chemistry in our bodies. It is a fact that the chemicals of stress dysregulate and downregulate our genes that create disease . . . if we can turn on the stress response just by thought alone and those chemicals can make us sick, then by very definition our thoughts can make us sick." E-Motion, Gaia.com, 2013

The realization that our thoughts and emotional baggage from our past can make us sick led me to energy work and my journey to heal myself through training as an energy healer. There are many techniques and aspects to energy healing but I will share some basic skills that others can easily learn and practise to create change and open awareness in their lives.

The first step in my training was learning to open my heart and feel unconditional love fully. As I learned to open my heart, connect to pure divine love and light, and practised various energy healing techniques, healing occurred. The power of love heals. Love is the basis of energy healing. A field of love in, on, and around the body lifts and removes the lower, heavy, dense energy of negative emotions from us. We feel lighter, more open, uplifted, and free. As a facilitator of energy healing, I now hold that field of love for clients to assist in their healing.

The second step in my training as an energy healer was to discover my own emotional patterns and, through various techniques, transform unhealthy patterns into healthier patterns through love. This meant accepting, honouring, and trusting what I could feel and see when I turned my attention inward and began observing myself. I learned that we memorize thoughts and emotions in our subconscious and they are stored in our bodies. I noticed that these emotional patterns in my body tended to be released in layers. For example, I was really angry and resentful at my husband and felt unsupported by him. As I transformed this emotional pattern by observing it, without judgement, I came to realize that I also felt angry and unsupported by colleagues, past friends, and all the way back to my parents as a small child. Each of these layers needed to be looked at, observed accepted and loved.

As I became aware that emotional patterns were stored in my body, I realized that I often recognized them as symptoms, tightness, pain or discomfort. Recognizing these sensations, I could connect to divine Love and Light, and focus on those painful, tight or discomforted parts of my body with unconditional love in those locations. Often that would release and transform those dense, heavy patterns into a lighter, more open and flowing energy giving me relief.

Sometimes just knowing where in the body wasn't enough to clear or transform that pattern. My soul wanted me to become aware of and have greater insight about that pattern so I could learn from it. If I recognized a tight or painful part in my body, I connected to a feeling of divine love and, with focussed intention, awareness and observation, I could ask questions. I could ask what emotions were stuck there or ask for any other insight. As I remained open to the insights it offered, the tightness or pain would often release itself. For example, I had a lot of disappointment, sadness and heartbreak in my chest area. That gave me insight to past trauma with my husband, old boyfriends, childhood friends, and my parents as a young child. I could then release and transform the whole pattern with unconditional love.

As I became aware of how emotional patterns work, I could use what thoughts or emotions were bothering me in the present and trace those emotional patterns back in time to find their cause and release them on an energetic level. For example, I often felt alone and lonely throughout my life. One day when I felt lonely, I asked where in my body I felt the pattern of loneliness. I became aware of and recognized a tight sensation in my chest.

I asked it questions like:

- Who did I pick up this energy from?

- How old was I when that happened?

- Are there any other emotions tied to it?

- Is there anything else I need to know?

I received the insight that I picked up that emotion from my mother when I was two years old. At that time, we had moved away from family to be with my dad who worked up north on the oil rigs. Mom was alone with me each day and many nights without family or friends to support her. That emotion was not even originally my own thought, but as a child I absorbed it from my mother and it was triggered many times throughout my life. With awareness and insight, I could then accept it and feel love again.

Each time a symptom developed, my body was communicating to me and showing me that something wasn't right. There was something that wasn't aligned with my own truth and authentic self, who I really am on a soul level. When I ignored the messages, my body escalated these messages to pain and illness until I finally started dealing with the emotional patterns that were stored there.

As I developed more awareness and skill, questions and insights became easier. In the beginning, when I asked questions, I may or may not have received answers to those questions. Sometimes they weren't the right type of questions, or I was thinking of or anxious about the answers I might receive. At the beginning, perhaps my awareness level was not opened or developed. I needed to trust myself for my intuition to develop further. Later I realized I may not need that insight to release the pattern. If I just set the honest intention, visualized and felt divine love, certain energies would dissipate even if I didn't know all the answers. More insight and answers came the more I believed and trusted that process.

Some of my symptoms included migraine headaches and, over time, my headaches progressed to sharp pains in my chest, which further progressed to a stress leave with major depression and anxiety. The medications and therapy I received didn't release my underlying emotional baggage from the past and my body further escalated it to cancer. This is literally what Summer described in the past section when referring to Dr. Sarnos' term, the Symptom Imperative. My body was literally screaming at me to acknowledge and deal with my past emotional patterns.

As I practised opening my heart and being connected to divine love and light, and practised identifying and releasing layers of heavy, dense energy of negative emotional patterns, I noticed my physical energy returning and my pain subsiding and eventually leaving. I no longer have chronic fatigue syndrome or fibromyalgia. My emotional and mental states started changing as well.

That negative ongoing chatter in my head, from my ego self who judged and put myself and others down, lessened and quieted. I set the intention to change my way of thinking and to change my perspective rather than listening to my ego mind. I could actually feel happy again. Glimpses at first, but as I kept transforming negative patterns and judgements into love, those happy moments extended and came more often. As emotional baggage from my past was lifted out of me, my soul-self emerged more and more.

My family life changed and I noticed how each of my family members started changing as I changed. My husband and I had been fighting for years and I had seriously considered a divorce. But as I released the anger and resentment I thought was toward him, I became aware of how it really came from my childhood. As I let those emotions go, our relationship healed. All of my relationships became healthier and I started becoming more open, honest and communicating more effectively. My confidence and self esteem levels dramatically increased. My whole personal vibration changed from low, dense, heavy negative energies of shame, guilt, anger, sadness, and blame to higher vibrational states of love, compassion, peace, gratitude, and taking full responsibility for the life I had created. I became happy about life again and learned to care for and love myself more.

An added bonus to removing my emotional baggage and tuning into love was that I started connecting more to my own inner wisdom and guidance, my own intuitive nature. I became more aware of my own truth and became more aligned to my authentic soul self. I can shine my light and love into the world in my own unique way. Now I have my own intuitive energy healing business where I help others apply what I have learned.

The magical element that produced all of this transformation is the energy of LOVE. We are all spiritual beings of love and light residing in physical bodies. This soul part of us is full of wisdom, peace, calmness, acceptance, and gratitude. It is the essence of our true, authentic self. This love is unconditional, non-judgemental and accepting of all that is – regardless of circumstance or situation. Each of us has this unconditional love within us. It is who we are on a soul level. It is the divinity that is within each of us. It just is.

These are big life transitions and wake-up calls. What each of these women had in common was a calling toward something more meaningful in life – a purpose beyond what they were currently experiencing and their emotional and physical symptoms were their calling cards. The pain they experienced stripped them down to their essence before they could live a more soul-aligned life.

What Migraines Can Tell You

Other wake-up calls come in all sorts of forms, one form is migraine headaches. Migraines, are specific and local to a particular immediate life situation or stress. They are painful and as a result, full of opportunity for expanded awareness. For example, I was at a health conference and a colleague came to me asking what I did for migraines. She was experiencing the onset of one and asked for my assistance. I explained some physical aids such as peppermint oil and lavender, but told her it was most important to explore an emotional reason behind the onset of the headache.

Being a hypnotherapist, she felt quite confident in her abilities to recognize her unconscious triggers, so we explored the physical energy to guide us there. I asked her to tell me the specific physical symptoms of the migraine. She explained the visual auras and the beginnings of nausea and that with this particular migraine, she felt it in her back.

Experiencing part of the migraine in her back was not a usual symptom, so I suggested we focus there. We could have explored the energy she felt in her back through the process of IN-OWT, but being in the middle of a conference hall, I went with my intuition and years of experience* that told me it may have to do with having a backbone and standing up for herself. As soon as I mentioned what I sensed the meaning of her back pain was, tears began to roll down her face.

"AHA!" I said. "I think we have just found the unconscious trigger for your migraine." She went on to tell me that she had just been in the conference hall and overheard someone speaking about her knowledge and information without crediting her for it and she had not said anything despite feeling a sense of betrayal. I suggested that she go lay outside on the earth, close her eyes and integrate this knowledge and decide what she wanted to do about it. Twenty minutes later, she returned to let me know her migraine had subsided. She felt back to normal and could resume her work at her booth.

As for myself, I had full-blown migraines into my late thirties. My last two migraines started the same way as all the others – numbness, nausea and visual impairment – but I was able to stop the progression by accessing the emotional prelude through the process of IN-OWT. From the first onset of the symptoms to the relief and feeling able to resume normal functioning, lasted no longer than two hours instead of three days. Most migraine sufferers can identify with my experience, but what they may not know is that with most migraines, there is an emotional prelude – an internal pressure that has built up.

A *headache* means that we are over-utilizing our head or thinking too much. It is a sign that we need to access our body's senses and engage other forms of awareness. The process of IN-OWT is a simple but effective way for accessing this awareness that has profound effects. For a more thorough explanation of INside-OWT, see Chapter 6, and you have access to how best to utilize the five steps in Chapter 7, the companion workbook to this book.

Simply put, the process requires that we remain present to the feelings and physical sensations the migraine presents, then accept, explore, and follow their trail to the underlying cause. Once we understand the nature of the conflict that precipitates the migraine by processing the emotions and thoughts that triggered it, the progression of the migraine stops. Yes, stops! The pain and nausea subside and deep, restful sleep follows. There are no torturous days of agony or the need to throw up.

* Please note, that in the beginning of my own awakenings, I did not trust my intuitions or even know how to distinguish my thoughts and mind from intuition. When people begin to work with the process of IN-OWT, it is natural to begin to build a sense of trust in one's intuition, visions, and in the overall process over time. Like anything, experience and practice builds confidence.

CHAPTER 3

The Health Scare System

What is Healing?

How I was shown the universal laws and principles of healing has a lot to do with my personal experience of life and work and what I knew *was not healing*. The idea or belief that we must fight or kill whatever invades our body, or cut out dysfunctional parts, is *not healing*. Instead it is a fear-based culture of care. Fear pervades our North American Health Care System, both on psychological and medical levels. As such, I refer to it as the *"Health Scare System."**

In the context of our Health Scare System, we are taught a veil or wall separates the body and emotions. There is psychology and there is the practice of medicine. One is for the emotions and the other for the body and the fear of their integration is high.

How did we end up here? Currently, the western globe's culture, science and medicine are founded upon the interpretation of Sir Isaac Newton's scientific discoveries. The portion of Newtonian Science that is used most rigorously – the scientific method – was and still is used without the sacred intent that Isaac Newton himself employed. Unfortunately, it was not his science that humanity embraced, but a truncated version of his thoughts that served to support those in power. In all likelihood, Sir Isaac Newton did not separate his science from the overarching power of Creation or of God. Sir Isaac Newton was first and foremost a theologian and a spiritual man. A man beyond his time and humanity, he was not ready for the all-encompassing reality in which he lived. Because humanity was not ready for his discoveries in their totality, their effects were only partially put to use. For more on Sir Isaac Newton, I encourage viewing of the DVD, *Newton's Dark Secrets* (2003).

Much of what he discovered was considered heresy and punishable by death. The truncated understanding of Newtonian science led to some advancements in medicine and physical well-being on many levels, but also created an:

> "inner psychological culture of speed, pressure and need for control – mirroring the outer culture of efficiency and productivity... People are in a hurry to know, to have answers, to plan and solve. We want more data, more ideas; we want them faster; and we want them ... to tell us clearly what to do. (Claxton 1997, p. 6)

Since Isaac Newton's laws of physics were formalized in 1687, our culture and science have been characterized by information gathering, intellect and impatience, which create an insensitive and hostile environment. "As we have come to seek and wield external power consciously, we have come to view feelings as unnecessary appendages, like tonsils—useless, but capable of creating pain and dysfunction. Thus, the pursuit of external power has led to a repression of emotion" (Zukav 1989, p. 60).

The deliberate avoidance or control of our innermost resources – our emotions and connection to the greater source of life – *is* insanity, but as a culture we have not yet recognized it as such.

Upon writing this book, I had a few of my favourite people tell me to avoid coining this term because it was inflammatory or might be offensive. I would like to clarify that by creating the term "Health Scare System," I do not mean that the current health system is not useful, only that one might recognize that it is ultimately a business and its marketing is, in fact, fear based. As for myself, if I break my arm or get hit by a bus, I use the medical system. I am not advocating an alternative to the medical system, what I am advocating is a form of complementary care. I advocate using and navigating all forms of care available to us when we are sick or unwell.

How Does the Mind Induce Physical Pain?

Although there are a number of ways the brain can induce symptoms in the body, Dr. Sarno says that the largest number of psychosomatic conditions can be tracked to the repression of emotion through the autonomic-peptide branch of the central nervous system (Sarno, 2006). Peptides are molecules that participate in a system of inter-communication between the brain the body.

Many types of physical pain are caused by mild and benign (meaning harmless) oxygen deprivation to a specific area of the body, and brought on by stress through the central nervous system. The activity of the *autonomic-peptide branch of the central nervous system* controls involuntary systems such as the circulatory, gastrointestinal, and genitourinary systems. It is active 24 hours a day and functions outside of our awareness.

> "The altered physiology in this process that creates the symptoms and physical pain appears to be a mild, localized reduction in blood flow to a small region or specific body structure, such as a spinal nerve, resulting in a state of mild oxygen deprivation. The result is pain. The tissues that may be targeted by the brain include the muscles of the neck, shoulders, back or buttons; any spinal or peripheral nerve and any tendon. As a consequence, the symptoms may occur virtually anywhere in the body." (Sarno, 2006, p.14-15)

Although it is true that symptoms arise anywhere in the body, in my experience the mind is not random in its choice of where or how the pain or symptom is experienced. Symptoms are often a precise metaphorical reflection of the underlying psychic, spiritual or emotional conflict the person is experiencing.

For example, as mentioned earlier, I suffered for years with excruciating migraines. In the past they proceeded into debilitating illness. White hot ice picks of pain ceaselessly thrust their way into my head, accompanied with left-side numbness, an inability to speak and waves of nausea that lasted for two to three days, until I threw up.

During my early 30s, one of my migraines affected vision in one eye and one side of my head. However, as I began developing my creative-intuitive skills and knowledge, I learned how to process the meaning and unconscious trigger behind the physical migraine symptoms. Processing pain through the laws of INside-OWT, allowed me to short-cut their effects. As I tuned into the energy of the migraine, I received the message that I had "turned a blind eye." I instantly understood what that meant to me. I acknowledged the conflict I felt because my husband insisted I work while my daughter was so young. During my migraine, the remorse and separation I felt when I left her in a day home surfaced. As soon as I set my mind to remove my daughter from daycare, the oxygen deprivation from the onset of the unconscious emotional conflict subsided and I quickly recovered. Now, I use the same process with others who experience migraines

> "These disorders afflict millions and cost the economy billions of dollars every year in medical expenses, compensation payments etc." (Sarno, 2006, p. 14)

The cost on the economy is large, but the human cost is greater. The cost to some, is their way of life. Similarly, some surgeries do more harm than good and the side effects of many types of pharmaceuticals are irreversible. Beyond the physical realities, social-emotional aspects keep many trapped in a perpetual cycle of illness that could be reversed through simple awareness and education.

When we experience some kind of physical pain, it is typical in our Western world to have a fearful thought, such as, "Something is wrong," "I'm sick," or "I'm dying," or "I might have cancer!" and "I need to 'fix this'." Now, imagine the kind of goose chase you can get into when you attempt to apply the medical model. The goose chase for some physical cause can keep people preoccupied, possibly obsessed with their physical health, and emotionally unconscious for years! Not many of us are prone to saying OH! I have a repressed thought or feeling, something I'm not paying attention to, and it's causing oxygen deprivation to *X* part of my body so I should ask it what's up!

This sounds remarkably simple, and in theory it is. Depending on the origin of the emotion on the time continuum of your life, often it really can be this simple. The work comes in undoing the layers of fear-based belief and familial patterns, if the symptom is familial and intergenerational. Symptoms, illness and disease that are embedded in the unconscious matrix of generations are a little more complex than a migraine brought upon by a local stressor, such as my daughter's chosen care provider. Nevertheless, the same process of discovery can unwind the stranglehold that our old ways of thinking have when carried on in the younger generations.

Our Outdated Mental Health Scare System

During my thirties, I trained at three and worked in two different hospitals. During one of my practicums for my masters program, I got a chance to develop and implement some Art Therapy programming on a psychiatric ward. Afterward I was hired and worked in a hospital specializing in healing after stroke.

My experiences at the hospitals were shocking and drove me clear away from allopathic and institutional medicine. The methods used in some wards of some hospitals are barbaric. Psychiatric units, dull and drug people and continue to use electric shock therapies. We might as well still behead, hang or torture people.

At the Psychiatric Unit

Early in my practicum on the psychiatric unit, I was aghast at some staff conversations. The unit was known as a *"revolving door"* because many of the same clients would return again and again. I'm sure, underneath the outside banter, some of the staff ultimately felt quite helpless. I'm quite sure they did not go into healthcare to see people harmed or sick or to be ineffective at preventing them from coming back.

I was invited to do some Art Therapy programming on this unit. My group included suicidal patients hospitalized for the severity of their thoughts and behaviours. Considering the depths of these patients' inner struggles, it seemed deplorable that there was no psychologist on staff. The goal was to assist clients in exploring different themes and aspects of their life and thinking, such as risk taking, control, grief, etc. I admired the raw authenticity of these clients, they had nothing to lose, nothing to hide anymore and I found it refreshing. They simply didn't give a shit!

I would like to share one simple, but profound, incident that occurred during one of our weekly sessions. On this particular day, with thick oil pastels, the patients were drawing how they were feeling. One client drew a black box, and immediately began experiencing a panic attack. As the patients were closely monitored, this person exclaimed their need to leave to get their anti-anxiety medication from their room. I asked gently where they might be feeling the sense of panic and the client immediately indicated that they felt it in their heart area. It appeared in their mind's eye as very black and this person began to breathe very quickly. I asked if I could touch their back and when they responded positively, I put one hand on their back between their shoulder blades (behind the heart) and asked them to breathe gently and watch.

Breathing, with their attention in the heart area, they watched. As they did, the black area in their minds eye turned to grey and, as their breathing slowed, it changed into a bright yellow! They were genuinely surprised by the shift and that's when they spontaneously remembered a repressed memory about their father. As there was no psychologist on the unit, one of the a full-time staff members found support for the client to pursue the integration of her memory and we purchased a couple of yellow shirts to remind them of the yellow, the hope and the release.

This opportunity to be present to their body and release a forgotten memory would have been lost had this person taken anti-anxiety medication to stop what was being experienced.

The African and Shamanic View of Mental Illness

The African or Shamanic view of mental illness is very different. In the shamanic view, Malidoma Patrice Somé says that mental illness signals *"the birth of a healer,"*

What the West views as mental illness, the Dagara people regard as "good news from the other world." The person going through the crisis has been chosen as a medium for a message to the community that needs to be communicated from the spirit realm. *"Mental disorder, behavioural disorder of all kinds, signal the fact that two obviously incompatible energies have merged into the same field,"* says Dr. Somé.

One of the things Dr. Somé encountered when he first came to the United States in 1980 for graduate study was how the West deals with mental illness. When a fellow student was sent to a mental institution due to "nervous depression," Dr. Somé went to visit him.

"I was so shocked. That was the first time I was brought face to face with what is done here to people exhibiting the same symptoms I've seen in my village." What struck Dr. Somé was that the attention given to such symptoms was based on pathology, on the idea that the condition is something that needs to stop. This was in complete opposition to his culture. As he looked around the stark ward at the patients, some in straitjackets, some zoned out on medications, others screaming, he observed to himself, *"So this is how the healers who are attempting to be born are treated in this culture. What a loss! What a loss that a person who is finally being aligned with a power from the other world is just being wasted."*

The Western world is not trained in how to deal with nor are they taught to acknowledge the existence of psychic phenomena or the spiritual world. Instead, psychic abilities are denigrated. When energies from the spiritual world emerge in a Western psyche, that individual is completely unequipped to integrate them or even recognize what is happening. The result can be terrifying.

Without the proper context for and assistance in dealing with the breakthrough from another level of reality, for all practical purposes, the person is insane. Heavy dosing with anti-psychotic drugs compounds the problem and prevents the integration that could lead to soul development and growth in the individual who has received these energies.

Excerpted from: *The Natural Medicine Guide to Schizophrenia, or The Natural Medicine Guide to Bipolar Disorder*, by Stephanie Marohn. (2003). Pages 178-189, Stephanie Marohn (featuring Malidoma Patrice Somé).

The chasm between the Western view of mental illness and that of earth based or Shamanic cultures, is vast. The shame, guilt and social stigma that comes from the Western viewpoint creates such a degeneration of the human spirit. To be fearful of symptoms that are normal and natural within a different paradigm of thought is, in my opinion, one of the biggest atrocities and wars taking place on our planet.

From Psychology to Humanology

Several of my friends and colleagues are psychologists, having worked with them during my training. Many recognize that psychology is not complete in itself and many take further training like Hakomi (body centred psychotherapy, Art Therapy, Play Therapy, EMDR, Somatic training, NLP (neuro linguistic programming), or many other supplemental modalities that engage a deeper level of mind and body than just talk therapy.

Many professionals recognize working with people requires a more compassionate human connection. Our system and governmental funding policies need to catch up to human evolution and the true needs of its citizens.

Once, when speaking to a 20-some-year-old with an addiction issue, I laughed uncontrollably when they told me their thoughts about the profession of psychology. In a very off-handed and casual way they said that "psychologists are paid to judge people". What made it so funny was that it's based in an undeniable truth. When working as part of a governmental institution, psychologists are mandated to diagnose and categorize according to the latest Diagnostic and Statistical Manual (DSM). If you have ever read one of these, you may notice that it provides a definition of disorders but does absolutely nothing in regards to what a) causes them, or b) what to do about them!

The DSM is simply a type of categorization most often used to slot people into certain areas of funding. Money and treatment is not provided unless people are given one of these labels. So, by applying a label to clients, people working for government institutions get paid. Unfortunately this creates another whole area of psychological anxiety. For many people, such labels promote low self-esteem and separation from the Universal level of their experience.

CHAPTER 4

The Apocalypse and the Quickening

Human Evolution

As we evolve as human beings, there are signs that our consciousness is being elevated to reveal familial or genetic patterns and untruths at an accelerated rate. There is a quickening, what some may call a crisis or an apocalypse happening in human consciousness. Apocalypse, from the Greek, means revealing truth or lifting the veil to disclose something hidden from humanity during a time of falsehood.

This quickening is leaving countless people experiencing illness, fatigue, emotional chaos, burnout and various ills and searching desperately for relief. For this purpose, people often seek answers from healthcare professionals, such as doctors, psychologists, massage therapists, naturopaths, chiropractors, and acupuncturists. Although we do have emotional and physical bodies that need care, the symptoms of the body, emotional or physical pain, negative thoughts or experiences, diseases, illnesses, or even accidents and injuries are invitations to look at and change your reality. As long as we refuse these invitations, our soul escalates the symptoms and the urgency of the invitation.

The Mind-Body Connection

Dr. Joe Dispenza, a neuroscientist immersed in the study of the mind-body connection, says that when people decide they want to make a change toward a better, more healthy version of themselves, they usually use about 5% of their conscious mind. As part of this 5% of conscious thought, things like positive thinking and affirmations are used. But, in order for change to take place, people need to start accessing unfamiliar and untouched aspects of the mind (Dispenza, 2014).

He says that your current personality creates your current personal reality. Going from the old self to the new self is a neurological, biological, chemical, hormonal, and genetic death of the old self and is a journey into the unknown that requires inner work. People can think positively all they want, but for change or healing to take place, you need to begin to access the other 95% of what is subconsciously held in the body and the mind.

If we don't start accessing the other 95% of the power of our mind deliberately, what I have witnessed is that this area of consciousness begins to ask to be acknowledged through the escalation of mind-body symptoms. The unconscious starts working its way out through the body. As people's minds and bodies break down, they are also breaking open to a new awareness. They are getting their wake-up call and beginning an inward pilgrimage toward the interrelated aspects of the mind, body and spirit. They are starting to have access to the other 95% of awareness.

This book is for those people who are willing to let go of fear and step into a new paradigm. For those who want to shift their awareness of their body and its physical symptoms from one of fighting, masking, numbing, or fixing the symptoms to one of interest, curiosity and trust! Honouring, accepting and trusting them as friends – YES friends!

Have you ever had a friend – a person who at first really irked or annoyed you and whom you initially avoided? Then one day, out of pure exasperation, you ended up accepting their invitation to some event and ended up becoming friends? This is what many of your body's symptoms are: dear friends and divine messages. However, our culture teaches us to see them as annoying and troublesome, or worse, to fear them. As a consequence, we judge them, avoid them, numb them, cut them out or fight them. Yet symptoms persist. You may overcome one illness and be riddled with another because your soul is trying to get your attention to relay a message. The energy of your soul often tries many different ways to get your attention (remember the *Symptom Imperative*) and waits for the right opportunity – the opening when you are ready to be present and willing to know.

Becoming Multisensory Humans - The other 95%

Gary Zukav believes the 5% of the brain we tend to use most often in the West is a byproduct of the intellect and used by the five-sensory personality to wield external power. Five-sensory personalities over-identify with the body's five senses (taste, smell, touch, hearing and vision) and thus pay attention to information that comes from external sources. Likely because many people have been so focused on external cues and senses, they recognize those five external senses but lump our internal senses into one broad category and call it the sixth sense. The sixth sense is further broken down by Zukav who uses the terms 'multisensory personality' and 'multisensory human' to denote people who attend closely to emotional currents and their heart-felt feelings as primary guidance tools.

> The central position of the heart in the higher order of logic and understanding of the multisensory human, and the sensitivity to emotional currents that is characteristic of multisensory humans, appear as extraneous to the five-sensory personality because they do not serve the accumulation of external power. ... Emotions are currents of energy that pass through us. Awareness of these currents is the first step in learning how our experiences come into being and why. (Zukav, 1989, p. 60-61)

Guy Claxton, in his book, *Hare Brain, Tortoise Mind,* describes this type of thinking – the 5% of data derived from the five senses that we use for logical problem solving – as d-mode (standing for deliberate or default mode). He says that,

> Deliberate thinking, d-mode, works well when the problem it is facing is easily conceptualized. ... But when we are not sure what needs to be taken into account, or even which questions to pose – or when the issue is too subtle to be captured by the familiar categories of conscious thought – we need recourse to the tortoise mind. ... This type of intelligence is associated with what we call creativity or even 'wisdom.' (Claxton, 1997, p. 3)

As a species, we are evolving into multisensory beings and starting to access the other 95% of our brain that connects us to a vast intelligence. I call the ability to tap into the creative wisdom of the mind the wave function. The wave function is an important concept in quantum science. D-mode and wave function are two complementary ways of perceiving and thinking.

It's much like the concepts of right and left brain, only it signifies much more than logical and creative thinking. It's about the creation of matter and physical form out of the realm of creative potentiality. In any given moment, we have a choice as to what to think and how to respond (wave function) but currently, human evolution and cultural values have us perpetuating choices based in past beliefs and e-motional patterns.

The instant we make an observation, a choice, or a judgment by thinking deliberately, using d-mode, the wave function collapses and the realm of potentiality closes into a single reality – that which we have manifested. These two ways of thinking or states of mind, d-mode and wave function, cannot be used simultaneously. It must be one or the other.

Here is the story of a woman, Olivia, who felt connected to her soul and easily accessed the wave function as a child, switched it off and lived in d-mode to be accepted, and eventually found her way back to living soul-side out.

My Journey Back to my Soul

Olivia Kachman - Fire Phoenix Dancer

As I stand from where I AM now in my life as a human being, I can see that every experience has taught me a valuable lesson. Every conflict, injury or trauma has inspired a deeper self-examination and opportunity to heal. Every heartache has broken me open to a truth I had yet to discover. Every situation that felt devastating at the time was designed to assist me in coming back home to myself – to my soul and my inner truth. I can see that now very clearly. It is not obvious when you are in the midst of the drama of your life, swept away by emotions or the pain of it all; however it is crystal clear when you begin to learn that you can choose to witness every experience, and see for the first time that life is not happening to you, it is unfolding <u>for</u> you.

Every single human being on Earth is orchestrating exactly the experiences they need to wake up to who they truly are. I truly believe that. It is through the hardships of the human experience that we are challenged to find our way to the other side of our wounds. No one can do this for you. You must do this for yourself! How do I know this? Every rebirth in my life, where I started over and recreated myself, demonstrated to me how powerful I AM as a creative free spirit who can manifest or be anything I desire. When I reflect on my life through this wisdom, I see many critical turning points in my life that either took me closer to who I AM and my soul, or took me away from it and resulted in some sort of crisis, pain, injury or upheaval. The situations that created this sense of separation from myself were really crucial for me to self-heal and come back to myself.

As a child, I absolutely loved exploring the expanse of forest acreage in my backyard. I spent hours of pure exploration, discovery, and adventure. Every ladybug and pine cone I held had a story. Every mossy nook invited dream time as I lay in its spongy bed. Every tree's branches that held me as I felt the wind sway the trunk, bending but never breaking, was deeply rooted. I could feel every stone was alive. I could see every leaf design was unique and, I observed that a fallen rotting tree was a home for all sorts of creatures living together. I could see that everything had a purpose and was important to everything around it. I was a pretty in-tune and gifted little girl! Life was simple and beautiful and I felt loved and safe.

Then one day, I had to go to school. The learning was less about discovery; we were told what we needed to know. Lessons started and ended abruptly when the teacher said, or a bell rang, not in the timing that my heart and soul wanted when I was so absorbed and in flow by an activity. We were told to do things a certain way, rather than our way, to always colour within the lines when we got older and should know better. My grade one school picture captured my discontent clearly like in passport photos when you are told not to smile. In school, we were rewarded for doing things the way the teacher wanted, and for the most part, we did what we were told. My parents also rewarded me for doing my best in school, and I thought they loved me more when I did well, so I started constantly proving how good I was, to earn their approval. They seemed so happy that I was smart, or good, or neat, or kind, so I just kept doing those things so they would love me and glow with praise and affection. I also wanted to be loved by others in my class. I clearly remember the day in grade three when the kids were talking about spiritual phenomenon like seeing ghosts or being psychic, and I thought everyone saw things and knew things! I soon was bullied as the freak weirdo kid, and I flipped the switch on my gifts turning them off completely. Two weeks later, I needed glasses because "I couldn't see anymore." My sensitivity to light and energy, psychic and intuitive powers, and clairaudience quickly faded away, and so did my eyesight. I began to drift away from my soul. I was seven years old.

These sorts of school experiences started a lifelong pattern of feeling I needed to prove myself by adapting to fit in, to be loved by others, and in my mind, love became something that was conditional and needed to be earned. By the time I entered the hallways of high school, the Latin motto, *adis quod agis* had become my life mantra: do well whatever you do. By this point, I accumulated awards for anything I set my mind to, which I later saw as the trophies I won for my parents' love and approval and not necessarily for myself. I had become driven by doing, competing, challenging, conquering. I jumped high, I ran fast, I moved gracefully, I wrote intelligently, and I accomplished incessantly. Nothing seemed wrong with that at the time, that was just the way things were in school. That was all I knew.

Proving my worth so people could love me became my unfortunate lifestyle. People praised me for being the amazing overachiever that I was, and that felt good at the time. Tragically, I had forgotten that I was a human being, not a human doing. I got swept away by the masculine energy of accomplishment, competition, action, and the disease of being busy all the time, and forgot about just being still with myself and honouring my soul. I was not listening to my inner compass, and my body was the first warning sign that I was going in the wrong direction. At the time I did not know that all my injuries were warning signs that something needed to change.

Movement has always been a natural gift of mine, and has always been integral to my Spirit. The joy and wellbeing I experienced as a child immersed in the forest was exactly how I felt when I danced! I loved the energy, the emotion, and the sense of flight and radiance when I danced. In junior high, I was introduced to volleyball.. It was a team sport and skill set I worked at with determination and diligence. For instance, I went from being benched by my high school volleyball coach to playing for both the city and provincial teams and training up to five hours a day. On a whim and a dare, I tried out for the University team that had just won a national championship, and to my surprise made the team! This was a major life crossroad: I needed to choose, between dance (my soul) and volleyball (my ego). My ego made the decision. Afterall, I was accepted to be on a team that just won its first National Championship! How could I pass that by?

When I blew out my patella in my second year in a practice and lay crippled on the gym floor gritting my teeth from the excruciating pain, I didn't realize that my injury was designed to get me to re-evaluate my life.

At the time, I did not know that issues with our knees represent our ego's desire to push forward, despite an underlying sense of inner conflict. I felt that my self-worth and identity were on the line so I stubbornly pressed on through the physical therapy and learning how to walk again. I was determined to be on the starting line-up of Team Alberta playing at Canada Games in five months.

I never did play in the starting line-up on the Canada Games team that year, and despite making the University team for my third year, I decided to move on from the relentlessness of proving myself as a volleyball player. It was just too hard on my psyche, and even more difficult on my soul.

My mother freaked out because her all-star athlete *quit* and this was hard to bear. I had let down my greatest fan and was now a disappointment. As a consolation prize, I tried returning to the dance group I left but the Russian ballet master told me I looked *too athletic*, then dismissed me with a wave of his hand. It felt like a door was slammed in my face. The nature of my injury and its consequences made me feel as though my life had ended. It took me 17 years to realize that all the panic attacks I experienced were symptoms of post traumatic stress disorder (PTSD), that had me experiencing the pain of this knee blowout, time and time again. Along with my knee, my ego had been completely shattered. Without being an athlete or a dancer, I did not know who I was anymore. I had defined myself by what I did. My whole heart and soul ached.

Another example of my body being a warning sign was when I broke three ribs. I fell in love with an Englishman while working abroad, got married and moved my whole life to his country. In doing so, I compromised myself completely. I soon discovered that I really did not belong in England. The lack of open-hearted people, the maze of bureaucracy, and my outgoing colourful character was foreign to the locals. I felt isolated.

Eventually, my husband wanted me to be more like the British women, rather than the free-spirited Canadian woman with whom he fell in love. Five years into our relationship, he changed his career direction. That's when I slipped in the shower and fractured three ribs. When he made no effort to take me to the hospital for care, I knew something was up. It made me question his love for me, and the truth came out – he had had an affair while he was in training and I had not seen it coming.

I could hardly breathe, feeling suffocated, stunned and in grief. I lay eight weeks bedridden, and this time I began to listen to my own inner knowing and wisdom. Within three months my soul guided me back home – to myself and Canada. I left my marriage, my teaching position in England, and the life I had there with my husband. This was an act of self-love. I learned that I need to remain true to who I AM always. I had unreasonably compromised myself and my whole heart and soul ached.

My injuries continued to transpire at other crossroads in my life. A debilitating elbow injury to my tendons occurred when I was incredibly unhappy in a toxic workplace in my new career as a photographer for a daily newspaper in northern Alberta, Canada. The subsequent therapy and counselling from this workplace injury revealed how I needed to leave my job, yet I felt like I had a purpose with my photography.

As I started to listen and tune into my soul, I was being called back to the child I was who enjoyed pure exploration, discovery and adventure. I felt that I was being asked to give a voice to the Earth and to capture the conflict of, "What we do to the Earth we do to ourselves." I began a mystical magical journey of actually listening to my soul's calling and how I was to use my skills and talents to make a difference. I had never lived like this before. It was exhilarating and rather scary to take this wild leap of faith, to use art as a means of expression and a call for social and environmental change.

I felt more in my power, and more myself, than ever before! My childhood gifts began to turn on again, and my intuition, sensitivity to energy, and qualities as an empath began to emerge in greater ways. I was supported by a compassionate and wise elderly woman, who held me and guided me as I stepped into this foreign territory within myself, and helped me to connect in the community and manifest all the resources I needed. She was a mystical-magical soul, and was not only a mentor, but an angel of a friend who came into my life just when I needed guidance. I felt so loved and supported.

I birthed an art installation from two years of photos, videos, and audio interviews. It was as though I was a vessel being used by forces much bigger than myself to create a meaningful work of art. Things just happened easily when I got out of my own way! I began to feel that I was on a spiritual journey, initiated by this heartfelt experience of deep listening to myself, to my intuition and other people I felt connected to. For one of the first times in my life, I felt I belonged in a meaningful community and felt a sense of co-creation. This entire experience was calling me home to myself, to my spirit, my soul and a deeper connection with the Creator.

My soul was calling me, and it had my attention. I began exploring some very deep parts of myself and was initiated into the world of Native Aboriginal spiritual practices. I was honoured to listen to many northern bush Cree elders in my time up north, and I was invited to my first experience of ceremony and sweat lodge. Within the steamy womb of Mother Earth, listening to the rhythm of the hand drum and the smell of sage, I felt so myself and a spark in my inner fire was ignited. There was something so familiar to the whole experience, it startled me. I remember once joining in the singing, and it was like I already knew the words of the song in Cree, and I had never heard Cree spoken before. Experiences like this became commonplace for me. I was literally led from one experience to another, meeting a key person with a message for me or another invitation, and I just started saying yes and showing up with curiosity and childlike wonder. Life literally was becoming magical – all my needs were met, resources flowed to me easily, different sorts of people and community groups were showing up in my life and teaching me exactly what I needed to know when I needed to know it. I was in the flow. I was finding my way home to my heart, each day was a new adventure, and I loved how it felt to be truly alive and in the moment.

I began the journey of lightening up, and I have not stopped. Enlightenment may not be what people think it is. There is no destination or finish line, but what feels amazing is being led by my heart and my soul rather than by societal expectations and social norms or pressures.

We need to make room for more light (literally) to come in. It is a process of feeling our emotions through to completion, letting go and remaining honest and authentic with ourselves and others. Even in the excruciating low dark nights of the soul and debilitating depression and anxiety, when I found my way back to my body, my heart and my soul, everything turned around for me. I have had to learn to surrender, to trust and have faith – lessons that I always come back to practising, when I need to find my way back to my Self.

Unveiling who I AM with more clarity and depth feels like the work I came here to do. I am a creative free spirit not designed for status quo or the conventional experience of 9-5, and likely neither are you. We are not meant to live a life restricted by the illusion of security of a solid job. We are meant to be fearless explorers and leaders, captains of our own ship. The human Spirit was never meant to be mechanized, systemized, clinically oppressed, or enslaved. The man-made societal constructs keep us distracted from our journey of honouring our soul's path.

Robert Frost said it best,

"I took the road less travelled, and that has made all the difference."

Robert Frost, *The Road Not Taken* (1916)

So where am I in this current moment on the journey?

I discovered that in healing my life, I was initiated as a healer and a way-shower. This began for me when I became a photographer after my failed marriage, and focussed on the beauty and wonder of the world through the lens of my camera. I became sensitive to light and emotion and the truthfulness of a split-second moment of our human experience. Photography healed my heart and my view of the world, and it activated the bold adventurer in me that was enraptured in the present moment.

I also returned to my passion for dancing, which eventually led me to ecstatic dance, where I literally shook every rule, restriction, and piece of choreography out of my cells, liberating my movement to the realm of the instinctual and intuitive. I began to tune into my body more and listen, and this started an incredible relationship with my body and all its signs, signals and messages. I read books, like Louise Hay's *You Can Heal Your Life*, and woke up to the fact that all my injuries and dis-ease were trying to tell me something. There was no coincidence that they all happened on my right side of my body – my blown out knee, my broken ribs, my elbow injuries – all were signalling to me that it was time to return to my more feminine nature.

I continued to follow my instinctual connection to aboriginal spirituality, and one day called in a teacher who could help me to better understand my own inherent gifts and wake them up again. An Algonquin medicine man was the teacher from whom I learned powerful energy healing and journeying through receiving medicine rites. Studying shamanism activated something in me that was already there. I discovered that my ancestral Ukrainian lineage was filled with healers, psychics, clairvoyants, mediums, and herbalists! It was all within me to begin with, and I am so grateful to discover this bloodline memory of my own ancestors through the teachings I have received.

With my passion for dance ignited again, I discovered Kundalini Dance, which was medicine for my mind, body and spirit. After a few life-altering experiences, I knew I was meant to share this with others and I became a certified facilitator. I literally have received an honorary qualification in somatic psychology from countless hours of observing how the body's intelligence, radar for truth, and phenomenal capacity to self-heal in myself and others. It has been a deep soul calling to empower others to realize that all the answers lie within, and that we are all our own best guru and healer when we learn to listen to ourselves – our bodies, emotions and our souls. Creating a safe and sacred space for people to connect and heal through vulnerability and a commitment to loving oneself completely have become my life purpose.

Receiving my medicine name, Fire Phoenix Dancer, from an elder, gave me the permission to follow my soul's purpose to bring beauty, truth and wisdom to people's lives, helping them to dance through the flames of transformation with a lightness in their step and a whole lot of grace! In embracing who I AM as Fire Phoenix Dancer, I have learned the power we have to heal and transform anything in our lives. In embracing the phoenix energy in me, which is about arising from the ashes of the first of life's experiences, I help others find the phoenix within themselves. Nothing is more satisfying to me than helping people to rebirth themselves anew!

This has been my journey of returning home to my soul, and it feels like it is only beginning!

It is my prayer that you too find your way home to your heart and soul, rebelliously galloping toward the horizon of your deepest heart's desires and dreams. If that is not clear to you yet, let the synchronicities be your guiding star, let your body's intelligence tell you what is true and what is not, and learn to follow and trust your instincts and intuition, as they always take you in the right direction!

As the quickening takes hold and propels people through their lives, more stories like Olivia's, Michelle's, and Jill's will emerge. It will become more common for us to see and understand the relationship between our physical existence and the realm from which it is formed. It will not be a smooth ride, but human beings will start to become increasingly skilled at recognizing and switching between the wave function and d-mode to become active co-creators of their experiences.

Multisensory Human - What it means to be a Light Being

What we are actually describing with these on/off states – from wave function to d-mode – is the nature of light. The two states – particle and wave – describe what quantum physicists call the wave-particle duality of light. Becoming a multisensory being also means that you are a being of Light and that you have the ability to both discern and navigate between these alternate states of being: wave or particle (d-mode). Children often access the wave function characterized by theta brain waves, which are associated with mental imagery, deep relaxation and meditation.

Unfortunately, for many of us adults, the important psychological resource of connecting to and using wave function has been severed with over-reliance or even obsession with d-mode and traditional research methods described as objectivity.

> Scientists have started to explore less deliberate ways of knowing through cognitive science ... What is becoming known is that, with time, unconscious realms of the human mind accomplish extraordinary and important tasks. ... These empirical demonstrations are more than interesting: they are important. For my argument is not just that the slow ways of knowing exist, and are useful. It is that our culture has come to ignore, undervalue them, to treat them as marginal or merely recreational, and in so doing has foreclosed on areas of our psychological resources that we need. (Claxton, 1997, p. 3-4)

For the first time in the modern world, the New Science and the spiritual mystics have the potential to come to mutual understanding of human reality. There is no denying that Larry Zukav's spiritual description of the soul and matter mirrors the quantum scientific concept of wave function and matter that Norman Friedman offers here.

> Matter is the form taken by consciousness when a probability selected from the hidden domain (of the wave function) is projected onto the level of space-time.

Thus mind and matter are aspects of a single reality. (Friedman, 1997, p. 136)

It has been determined by quantum science that the observer of any experiment (e.g., your life) affects the outcome of the experiment – NO MATTER WHAT. The universe does not use the scientific method nor does it believe in the separation of objective or subjective realities.

> The words "objective" and "subjective" are illusionary, a misinterpretation of the mind based on a level of consciousness that is evolving. Traditionally, research has been built upon a classical Newtonian approach where the observer or researcher was an external agent who was considered to be totally neutral and objective. Nowadays, we believe that the observer is always involved in the process of observing and, in spite of his or her best efforts to the contrary, will always influence the (research) and its eventual outcome. In a participatory universe, there is no such thing as a neutral observer. According to quantum theory, not only is the observer involved, but the observer actually brings about what is being observed. (O'Murchu, 2004, p. 33)

Norman Friedman puts it this way.

> There is no objective reality underlying our everyday world except when it is being observed (i.e., chosen). We do not know what state a system (person) is in before measurement, it must be in a superposition of all possible states." (Friedman, 1997, p. 57)

Thus, everyday, our personality has a choice from a multitude of possibilities and states through access to the wave-function. What d-mode does, is observes and chooses a potential state and in its choosing, it takes it out of potentiality into material reality, i.e., manifestation of the chosen reality. As human beings, we do not realize that we are continuously choosing because we are predominantly in d-mode, making many of the same choices, over and over again. We are participating in an energetic pattern and have either forgotten or never learned how to interrupt these patterns by navigating between d-mode and wave function. Developing the relationships between soul and personality is the key lesson of the next few decades.

There is no better demonstration of these distinct states of mind, d-mode and the wave function, than Jill Bolte Taylor's video on *Ted Talks*, "My Stroke of Insight." As a neuroscientist, she retells the story of the day she suffered a massive stroke to her left cerebral hemisphere. She clearly recalls her experience of how her d-mode processing cycled on and off and when her wave function kicked in. When her wave function (or right hemisphere) was on, she found herself immersed in a reality whereby she experienced the oneness of all there is and the inability to discern the separation between the particles of her body and that of a table or an apple for example. I highly encourage the reader to watch this Ted Talk before reading on.

The Role of the Wave Function

As Jill Bolte Taylor experienced and so clearly articulates in her video, our mind has two main functions, modes, or on/off states. Our d-mode allows us to make logical linear or particle like steps and the wave function allows us to understand that we are connected to, and one with, all that is.

> The creation of physical experience through intention, the infusion of Light into form, energy into matter and soul into body, are all the same. The distance between you and your understanding of the creation of matter from energy is equal to the distance that exists between the awareness of your personality and the energy of your soul. ... The system is identical. (Zukav, 1989, p. 130)

The relationship between a soul and the day-to-day reality of the personality is an important aspect of awareness. A useful metaphor is to view the soul as a conductor that manages energy between the circuits of the universe and the personality. The personality is the grounding medium of the soul. However, for many people, they are not aware of their soul, and therefore not aware of its role in grounding the energetic information that the soul imparts.

Believing in an objective reality may have simplified life, but has limited our human potential. Belief in objectivity limits possibility and by doing so we reduce the creative exuberance of God's Spirit to a personal projection of our own making, and in the process violently disrupted the flow of life in both planetary and personal terms. (O'Murchu, 2004, p. 31)

Having access to the wave function and Universal consciousness, makes us aware that we are part of one energy, one matrix of human consciousness intermingled with a divine presence. When we are at one with this presence by accessing the wave function, and we give ourselves permission and time to belong to it, we heal. I say we because as individuals accessing the wave function and healing our personal lives, we become instrumental in healing the collective aspects of our experience at the same time.

We have collectively and unconsciously chosen certain realities as a culture that are difficult to see and observe because we are so accustomed to seeing them, that we are unaware there are other possibilities. Being in d-mode restricts our understanding that there are choices. D-mode is fear based and limited in scope, time and space. The choices we made, and the cultural and societal ones we have unconsciously accepted, seem static and perfectly normal and real, because it's been familiar to us for so long (usually our whole life.)

I do not believe you are 100% individually and independently responsible for your life's circumstances because you have likely been unaware of the energetic matrix you belong to, it's laws and how to navigate it's realm. However, once you are aware of the matrix, the laws, and the ability to tap into the knowledge to navigate it, you are granted 100% of the power to effect change and are responsible for doing your part in making the shift to greater health and well-being. If you do not own your knowledge or make excuses for procrastinating, ignoring or denying, you will quickly find yourself in physical or emotional pain, which is just a reflection of the pain of separation and disconnection the matrix feels without your unique and essential contribution.

The energetic experiences and choices you make while you access the realm of the wave function allows you to effect personal change, but also to affect the energetic matrix and change the realities for all affected by the same energetic mis-alignments. You can choose to become an empowered being.

The Role of Fear

When people are unaware of their relationship to their soul, or that of the collective reality, a person becomes over-identified with the transient qualities of their personality, which produces an inevitable and underlying emotion of fear. The personality can't see possibility or choice because in d-mode the world appears stagnant, closed and solid. The irony is that the personality or d-mode thinking is incapable of understanding or seeing its way through the emotions that fear produces. It's a self-fulfilling cycle.

> The fearful and violent emotions that have come to characterize human existence can be experienced only by the personality. ... Only the personality can judge, manipulate and exploit. Only the personality can pursue external power. The personality can also be loving, compassionate and wise in its relations with others, but love, compassion and wisdom do not come from the personality. They are experiences of the soul. (Zukav, 1989, p. 30)

Let's break down the word emotion: e-motion. The letter e stands for energy and motion means movement; emotions, therefore, are energy in motion. As Gary Zukav says, "emotions are currents of energy that pass through us" (Zukav, 1989).

Emotions, can be properly discerned and understood only from the perspective of our wave function. It is the wave function that understands continuous movement, otherwise emotions seem illogical! E-motions are not particle-like in nature therefore we cannot use d-mode to process them. As soon as we use d-mode, we begin breaking the information into static units, which stops the motion. Only the wave function can access the meaning of emotion and connect us to the force field of our soul.

Exploring and understanding the feelings and thoughts behind our emotions is not well mapped in conventional Western psychology or spiritual traditions. Certainly, exploring our inner world and honouring its reality as equal to that of physical reality is, for some, not only unconventional, but a ludicrous proposition. Thus, our inner images, emotions, intuitions, dreams, and perceptions are discouraged, passed over as insignificant and, in a number of ways, treated with insensitive hostility or violence. Because we are taught to avoid, mistrust, and repress this information, most of our inner world is governed by our shadow – what we are unaware of, cannot see or don't want to see within ourselves.

Anything that gets in the way of light creates a shadow. In other words, a shadow is the absence of Light, the absence of divine energy, the absence of soul. Ultimately when we make friends with our shadow, with our darkness, it is not scary. Rather, it is only a part of us seeking to become known, to be illuminated and to be loved.

> What we call evil is the absence of Light, of love, in all cases. ... How we understand evil, therefore, is very significant. Evil needs to be understood for what it is: the dynamic of the absence of Light. ... Understanding evil as the absence of Light automatically requires that we reach for this thing called Light. ... The remedy for an absence is a presence. Evil is an absence and, therefore, it cannot be healed with an absence. By hating evil, or one who is engaged in evil, you contribute to the absence of Light and not to its presence. (Zukav, 1989, p. 69-70)

As the universal shift takes place and people experience the quickening, it is natural for pain and suffering to become intolerable before the personality becomes willing to seek authentic power as generated through the soul. The purpose of the pain is to push the personality through the fear and toward the journey to becoming a multisensory being.

Because the personality cannot discern the meaning of emotions, symptoms, or connect to the soul using d-mode, it needs to learn how to understand the soul's language. In learning to tune into and learn the language of the soul, the wave function, an increasingly intimate relationship between the personality and the soul can develop.

The Universal Language of the Soul

Oral and written languages reflect the societal beliefs and values of the era in which the language develops. The soul's language, on the other hand, is consistent across time. It is timeless and energetic. Sufi Mystic Hazrat Inayat Khan calls the soul's language Cosmic Language (Khan, 1972). Jeanne Achterberg describes it as a preverbal or *a priori* language. *A priori* means a language that has always existed. It is a language we all possess when we are born, a language of archetypal images, symbols and feeling. It is a language that speaks of the deep interconnection and purpose of mankind.

It is preverbal in a sense that it probably evolved much earlier than language and uses different neural pathways for the transmission of information... Here, the imagination acts up on one's physical being. Images communicate with tissues and organs, even cells to effect a change. The communication can be deliberate or not. (Achterberg, 1995)

The soul's language contains information based on rhythm and pattern and enables us to make discontinuous leaps or what seems like abstract or random connections based on wave patterns of energy rather than on particle-like step-by-step connections. The energetic language of the soul, or the wave function as it implies, is about connected movement – ripples and undulations of interconnected energy. It encompasses many forms within the body, including body sensations, pains, twinges, flutters and all kinds of symptoms, internal sound and voices, and inner images. They can happen while awake or dreaming, and comprise memories, colour, light, rhythm, movement, dreams, and automatic dialogue – words that spontaneously impart wisdom.

Mind-body symptoms – our way of being in the world, of thinking and feeling – is a result of the meaning we attribute to our life experiences. To get a deep understanding of who we have become and why, we attend to the meaning of our experiences, which is most evident through the energetic language of the soul and accessible through metaphor and imagery. Every object, animal, situation or encounter has an energetic vibration with a specific frequency, which gives each thing a specific purpose. "The universe and everything in it 'is' what it 'is' because of the force of consciousness itself, our beliefs and what we accept as the reality of our world" (Braden, 2007, p. 8).

The soul's language is rich in metaphor. Metaphors imply meaning by comparison and invoke layers of meaning and feeling. For example, in being stuck between a rock and a hard place, or being told, "You are a such peach," or "I feel like a volcano about to explode," rock, peach and volcano are English Language labels for these objects. But, whatever language label you use, whether it be in French, Spanish, German, etc., the understanding or feeling of each object, is very similar.

Again, it is not about trying to understand the metaphor of your symptoms and being logical using d-mode. The language of the soul is naturally and effortlessly energetic. As we access the wave function, we are presented with symbols and images that are keyed into our personal experiences. "Images, indeed all thoughts (and feelings) are electrochemical events, which are intricately woven into the fabric of the brain and the body" (Achterberg, 1985, p. 9).

It is no coincidence that we are presented with symbols and images that reflect our internal experiences. The universal system of light and our consciousness are precise and fluid. Sometimes people see certain types of people or symbols or numbers over and over again during certain times of their life. This is why Spirit Animals, which are an energetically metaphorical mirror for the energy within your soul, are REAL – they are a precise reflection of your energy.

Arnold Mindell explains:

> ... when you work on your symptoms, don't just try to heal them. Focus on learning about their unknown inner realms, on awareness practice, experimenting with using your awareness in different ways. Coming to a particular conclusion or insight is helpful, and interesting, but what usually influences symptoms is the awareness practice itself – your access to your own hyperspace, your expanded sense of reality. Developing moment-to-moment awareness leads you toward an increasingly congruent lifestyle. You become more of who you are. (Mindell, 2004, p. 58)

On a psychological and spiritual level, knowing we can access the wave function, and learning how to do so, has a profound effect on our lives. Physicist David Bohm added a psycho-spiritual dimension to quantum physics when he re-conceived quantum waves in terms of what he called pilot waves (Bohm, 1980). Arnold Mindell utilizes Bohm's concepts and their implications widely throughout his work as a psychotherapist. He suggests that the wave function is a guiding force that informs particles where to go and with altered states of consciousness can emerge as an insight that may be connected to a physical symptom. Mindell states:

> As the subtle experience arises, it flirts with your attention. It appears as a slight sensation, wiggle, thought or pulse-like form ... You can imagine how, if ignored, this essence experience of the force of silence (wave function) can become a perception, feeling or dream image. Finally, if this is ignored, it may eventually appear as a visible signal or noticeable symptom (Mindell, 2004, p. 51).

As human beings evolve into multisensory humans, we learn to encompass the senses that come from within – the non-physical qualities of energy. The universe is keyed and coded to impart meaning and the mysterious nature of the wave function. Bringing "something into being or form out of nothing – is an enigma until you recognize that nothing also means no thing. Creation is bringing form out of transcendent possibilities that are not things" (Goswami, 1999, 82).

The guidance at the end of this book, the 10 Universal Laws of Healing, will support you in adjusting to the new perspectives and belief structures you need to access your wave function and your soul's language. The five steps of the acronym INside-OWT lays out the natural process stages that bring about the progression of soul language and spontaneous insights. Finally, the workbook section of the book prompts you in how best to practise and utilize these steps to witness yourself or others' inward journeys.

The workbook has key ideas and scripts for enabling and bringing about the free-flowing and spontaneous imagery and insights the wave function inevitably brings about. The wave function allows us as individuals and as a species to transcend our old belief structures and wounds, and enter a field of endless possibilities. The workbook helps you take wave function information and implement it into your life through your personality.

The major difference between this process and other types of psychology, counselling, meditation, or hypnotherapy is that both the client and the witness – what I call the mentor – benefit from the process. It is a mutual adventure and as we learn to trust the energetic map and follow the energy trail it lays out, the wave function moves freely toward your highest good and that of all. All whom are witnesses (I teach groups) are served by the transformative energy. What uplifts the one, uplifts all. We are all a part of the universal network and collective awareness.

Immerse
yourself in your inner being

Notice
what comes up

Own
what is presented

Willingness
to play and accept the metaphorical processes

Trust
that you are safe & guided

CHAPTER 5

Healing from the INside-OWT

IN-OWT (Immerse. Notice. Own. Willingness to Play. Trust.), or INside-OWT is the acronym that provides the structure of a timeless, energetic language we've forgotten and are beginning to remember. IN-OWT is a fluid five step process – a way of communicating that accesses the wave function. The purpose of the process is to enable the personality to understand and integrate the information our soul is imparting into our lives. It can be used in conjunction with other types of healing modalities or counselling practices to deepen awareness and integration.

IN-OWT is a natural process that follows laws I became aware of and am simply putting into words. It is a way to articulate in English all I know and understand about the infinite source of inherent meaning that we activate by living our lives authentically and truthfully.

Lots of healing modalities, creative expressions and types of meditations have tapped into some aspect of the soul's language. The quickening is asking us to take deep dives and accept radical response-ability, that is, the ability to respond and implement the philosophy and apply it. This can be challenging. There are so many other worldly lures to attract our personality and distract our attention. I call it the attract and distract rule.

Dispenza gives a reason we are so easily distracted and why it is difficult for us to pull our attention away from all of the conditions of our outer world and tune into our inner world.

> Most people are addicted to stress hormones – to feeling the rush of chemicals that are the result of our conscious or unconscious reactions. This addiction reinforces our belief that our outer world is more real that our inner world. And our physiology is conditioned to support this, because real threats, problems and concerns do exist and that need our attention. So we become addicted to our present external environment. And through associative memory, we use the problems and conditions in our lives to reaffirm that emotional addiction in order to remember who we think we are. (Dispenza, 2014, p. 151)

Often, by the time people come to see me, they've been attracted and distracted for so long, they are already on extended sick-leave or disability of some form, engaging a full-blown health crisis or depression and with a long list of people they have seen for desperate relief.

Allowing the old self to transform into the new self is very much like performing internal surgery. Remember, Dr. Joe Dispenza calls it a *neurological, biological, chemical, hormonal and genetic death of the old self* (Dispenza, 2014).

Because of the nature of our culture, most people are unequipped or afraid to allow the death of the old self and miss the opportunity to transform and heal. Not only do you need to trust and allow this emotional, spiritual and genetic death to occur, which really only means letting go of what no longer serves you, you need to trust the unknown and rebuild by interpreting the soul's messages. Remember, the body is a divine conduit of the soul's energy – you need to know how to conduct the energy without it short-circuiting. To understanding the soul's language, the wave function is imperative. Your body, mind and spirit knows how, it's a natural process, we just forget.

Until now, because our society is focused on the five senses, when the physical body is unwell people take sick leave. Most people won't often admit to taking a personal mental leave, but nothing could be healthier. For the purposes of letting go of the old self or, in essence, performing "internal surgery" as Joe Dispenza suggests we must recognize it is worth the time and self-care it requires. It is of great benefit to take a period of time - usually 3-6 months on a health leave, sabbatical or modified work plan for the purposes of reconnecting with our inner life. Compared to the amount of time people suffer, usually years, the time for getting a firm grounding on a healing path is relatively short especially with a skilled mentor or teacher who can assist you.

Taking time like this may seem extreme or unnecessary in our retail-numbed western reality but ancient cultures have initiations that bring you to this point of spiritual development deliberately.

It is about becoming a multi-sensory person. It's about learning through the process of life and opening possibilities of profound transformation and healing. Some call it manifestation or the law of attraction, which it is, but it is also more than that. Your life view may be seriously challenged or you may be sick enough to want to emerge through gripping fear that the world and who you are in it doesn't work anymore. This IS the Apocalypse. It is happening within many of us.

The Role of Truth

This shift is NOT about positive thinking!

When beginning to integrate the 10 laws that enable us to use INside-OWT to its fullest capacity, it must be emphasized that this does not mean using positive thinking to try to be healthy or in harmony when we feel we are not. To choose and identify with a perception of life that aligns us with our soul and with health and harmony, means accepting what one feels, loving what is, accepting truth, and identifying its meaning within. Only then can incongruent thought patterns be changed to realign with one's soul and can new action be taken through the personality.

> To heal the limits of either a conscious or unconscious perception/belief, we must somehow bypass what the mind has believed in the past and replace it with something new based in an experience that is true for us: our inarguable truth. (Braden 2007, p. 163)

Positive thinking is often about the way you think things *should* be and often people end up denying what actually *is*. Truth is not our perception or judgment of a person or situation, or a wish or an idea of what it could be; truth just *is*. There is a situational truth about a situation, e.g., whether or not your spouse is having an affair or is an alcoholic, and then there is the energetic truth and the lesson in any given situation. When you are ready to ask with earnest inquiry, your feelings and e-motions tell you the truth immediately. Your wave function can take you back years of energetic patterning - of your own - and your familial patterns that can be revealed to you. The why of any given situation has a lot to do with life-lessons and spiritual mis-alignment.

When my clients tell me about their affirmations or attempts at positive thinking, I simply ask if they actually *FEEL* the statement is true or not. Often, the answer is no. When people are trying to force a positive feeling out of forced thinking, it is actually a judgment and a form of violence toward oneself. When you are using positive thinking to deny what is, you are using d-mode to try and force that positive feeling – which is a judgement, not truth and keeps many people stuck in their realities.

Truth serves our growth and the development of our soul. Byron Katie, a woman who experienced what she calls a "waking up to reality" in 1986 explains truth in her book *Loving What Is*.

> The only time we suffer is when we believe a thought that argues with what is. ...We can know that reality is good just as it is, because when we argue with it, we experience

tension and frustration. We don't feel natural or balanced. When we stop opposing reality, action becomes simple, fluid, kind and fearless. (Katie, 2002, p. 1-2)

When people begin this type of journey into accepting, honouring and trusting what is, some still judge what they experience. They often switch back into d-mode. However, as people begin to get familiar with the wave function and connect to their Inner Knowing, they learn to trust. Eventually clients stop trying to out-think, judge, or deny the truth and this frees a tremendous amount of life-energy. Positive feeling, as opposed to positive thinking, means that we can actually feel the movement of energy and the outcome we desire as being set into motion. This is truth.

The Human Battery

Our body is like a battery with positive and negative poles. Instead of taking it for what it is – a negative or positive charge – we have labeled these energies as good feelings (positive) or bad feelings (negative). If we feel happy or excited (positive) we think that's OK, if we feel grief, resentment, or depletion (negative) often, many of us tend to get busy and avoid these feelings. We justify them, hide them, deny them, stuff, them, repress them, judge them, and we think of affirmations or try to force positive thinking (with the intent of making the bad feelings go away!)

As humans we've been taught to identify with one pole of e-motion, the positive, and disassociate from or deny the negative. The consequence of this is that our battery stops working. If we block, stop, deny, or repress negative feelings or pain, we can't learn from them. We prevent the battery's natural energy flow that cycles between negative and positive. Our energy begins to stagnate and we become ill.

So it is, in the struggle and hyper-intention to be happy or successful, we bring about more of our own unhappiness, illness and perceived failure. Ironically, happiness, health and well-being happen when you don't focus on trying to achieve them. For success, like "happiness, cannot be pursued; it must ensue, and it only does so as the unintended side-effect of one's personal dedication to a cause greater than oneself or as the by-product of one's surrender to a person other than oneself." (Frankl, 1984, p. 17)

As an individual with a soul, we are intricately woven into a larger human energy field. It is d-mode and the personality, not the soul, that judges e-motion. From the Universe's perspective, neither the positive nor the negative magnetic charges of energy are preferred; rather they are necessary and complementary principles of the universal system of light.

> There is a huge difference between 'judging' these forces and discerning that they exist and what they represent. And it is in this subtle yet significant distinction, that we find the secret which allows us to rise above the polarity and heal the conflict between light and dark. (Braden, 2007, p.127)

As a complementary electromagnetic system, there is a perpetual degree of tension or polar energy between the soul and personality that compels a person to seek out and birth new perspectives and possibilities. It is an ever-evolving process, not a static one, in which there exists, "a polar field of tension, where one pole is represented by a meaning that is to be fulfilled (one's soul), and the other pole by the man (personality) who has to fulfill it" (Frankl, 1984, p. 127).

Each soul is a unique energetic system contributing to the ever-unfolding process of Creation through the actions brought forth and implemented by the personality. The choices a person makes at each moment contribute to what they become and to the health of the energetic system between the soul and personality. Our personalities and our bodies die, but the energy of our soul cannot be destroyed, only transformed. Thus, the energy of our soul travels through lifetimes.

If we are to engage the viewpoint of the soul, we must cease from judging, even those events that appear to be unfathomable such as the cruelty of inquisition or a holocaust,... we do not know what is being healed in these sufferings. (Zukav, 1989, p. 44)

Energetic patterns of incongruence and disharmony stay with us until we learn their lessons. The tasks of the next millennium require a substantive shift in human consciousness to become sustainable. We will require new perspectives and new actions with which to live in harmony with each other and the natural world. IN-OWT is a way to trust the development of your multisensory faculties that, I believe, your health and the health of the planet depend upon.

Becoming the Cosmic Artist of Your Life.

If your life were a painting, creating your life in d-mode is like a paint-by-number. Creating art in this way – with a predetermined end product – is more of a craft or a manufacturing process. True art is healing. True art is a process whereby time ceases to exist and energy is transformed. Gregg Braden calls this process becoming the *"Cosmic Artist"* of your life (Braden, 2008).

As the Cosmic Artist of your life, you are able to engage the sacred process of creation by accessing the wave function and learning the language of the soul. By doing so, we are "expressing our deepest beliefs on the quantum canvas of the universe" (Braden 2008, xx), and as we engage this sacred process, "we learn that the process has an intelligence that can be trusted" (McNiff, 1992, p. 21).

I often use art and painting with clients to engage the wave function. The IN-OWT principles can be used and applied to almost any activity or healing modality. Using the principles of IN-OWT in a soulful painting process (without the therapeutic analysis or typical gallery assessments of art as a commodity) is one way to access the wave function and the healing it can offer. Paint is a useful tool for accessing the wave function because it's so fluid and flexible. It's so difficult to control, that the resultant frustration it presents if you are in d-mode is a clear guide to refocus your attention.

Frustration is easy to develop during the process of painting if you do so in d-mode and try to manufacture a specific end product or image-type. Creativity and the act of co-creation is not about what you already know or copying images that already exist; it's about venturing into the unknown and creating something surprisingly new. This is the essence of the wave function and the Universal undulating vortex of Source energy we can access.

Peggy's Story – Painting from the Soul

My friend and Colleague, Peggy Funk-Voth, a Jungian analyst and clinical social worker by profession, shares her story of healing during a soul-painting session.

At one point in my life, I developed an inflamed rotator cuff and frozen shoulder through repetitive motions while working out at the gym. When medical interventions didn't work, I turned to alternative therapies. All of these professionals I saw told me that I was carrying anger in my heart. This surprised me because I didn't *feel* angry. I *never* felt angry. I could not identify any flicker of anger within myself.

In hindsight, this can be explained by the fact that I grew up in an environment in which anger was bad, unacceptable, a sin. This belief was deeply socialized into me, disconnecting me from a primal source of information *(and energy)* that, it turns out, I desperately needed. Not surprisingly, while all the help I sought benefited me in other ways, it did not touch my pain-filled rotator cuff, my almost-useless, dead-weight left arm.

When a group of friends invited me to a Soul-Paint Workshop facilitated by Summer, I decided to go. Never having painted before, I felt a lot of trepidation. I went in order to be with my friends, none of whom were artists or painters.

As I tried to copy a scene based on the picture I had chosen to bring as inspiration, I froze. I was horrified by my poor replication *(judgment and fear)*. Anxiety filled my body. Summer gently turned my inspiration picture face-down, led me into slow deep breathing, then guided my hand in covering the canvas with white paint. "Now trust, choose a colour and feel free to make big, expressive strokes," she said, releasing my hand. I did this several times, covering the white canvas with horizontal strokes of pink, green and blue.

Summer stayed near, giving me permission to do things my way, encouraging me to move beyond my comfort zone *(moving beyond fear)*. As I began to relax, she merged into the background, yet came forward to offer support at crucial points in my process. I felt emotionally safe *(feeling safe and switching to wave-function)*.

Suddenly, I wanted to PAINT. I took a brush in each hand and brushed vertically with both hands. As I eased into trusting *(trusting the process)* the movement of the paintbrushes, a sensation of warmth spread through my chest on the left side where my heart is.

The warmth built and intensified until it was hot. It then filled my left shoulder (the one with the inflamed rotator cuff) and began to move into my arm. Heat crept down my upper arm, turning it hot. Heat inched past my elbow, suffused my forearm. Then the fire flowed free, into my hand, through my fingers, and burst out of my left brush. The colours turned angry. Each stroke became heavier, thickening and darkening the colours, while my right-handed strokes engaged in a more delicate dance.

As the hot energy dissipated, I began to feel lighter, freer and more playful. I picked up a clean brush, dipped it in white paint, and flicked the bristles at the painting, creating white-hot sparks.

That event marked a turning point in the healing of my rotator cuff. The inflammation began to decrease. Blood was able to flow into the tissue, cleansing it of toxins and repairing it with oxygen and nutrients.

The painting experience *(access to the wave function)* unlocked my physical lock-down and opened the way for other therapies to work more deeply. My shaman took me into the in-utero and birthing situations that activated protective patterns so that I could survive psychologically. My energy worker brought an understanding of the rage I carried; it was collective and archetypal, giving it a power and meaning that was beyond personal. My massage therapist provided visualizations that helped the cleansing work of blood-flow to continue between sessions.

It turns out that I WAS angry. And my anger was not bad. In fact, it brought direction to my life. I began to explore the collective and archetypal rage that had taken up residence in my heart.

Like Peggy, I believe we are all angry and we should be! As good citizens, we repress our anger.

Anger is a natural response to the repression and disconnection from our Soul life. We have been culturally and unconsciously led into a collective war-like behaviour toward ourselves. Judging emotions and feelings without a clear direction of how to utilize their energies, they go inward and create debilitating symptoms just like Peggy's.

We are soldiers, like zombies, when we live life from d-mode and from outside expectations imposed by the cultural values of our age. Peggy's example of the release of anger and resultant healing isn't a miracle.

"Miracles are not contrary to nature. They are only contrary to what (we think) we know about nature."

St. Augustine, AD 353 (Oyle, 1976)

Using the knowledge of the five steps inherent to IN-OWT with the medium of paint, allowed access to the wave function. The wave function is that aspect of our being that releases energies in their particle state so that they may be released back into the realm of possibility. At one point in Peggy's life, she made a judgment about her anger toward herself and her relationship to the world that resulted in holding that energy in a particle-like state, i.e., without movement. As a result, it manifested in her body as a frozen shoulder. This is unfortunate in that it locked the potential movement this e-motion could have in leading her in the direction of her soul's path. The neat thing about decisions we make to repress or judge aspects of ourselves and their energies, is that they wait. It is in particle state, until we choose for it not to be. Symptoms are willing and ready to accept our invitations to re-enter the wave function and allow the Universal matrix to transform it out of its frozen (particle) state, whenever we are ready for something different to take place.

The wave function allows the energies out of the body and their frozen d-mode state. Peggy's example is the epitome of Dr. John Sarno's work described in Chapter 3 and of how the mind unconsciously creates physical pain in areas such as muscles, joints, and tendons, through mild oxygen deprivation initiated by the autonomic-peptide branch of the central nervous system, when we deny or repress certain emotions. Peggy's personality took ownership of her rage and began applying the knowledge to her life. Her exploration took many forms.

The exploration of my rage came through reading, conversations, connecting the dots of occurrences in my life, and spontaneous visions. I have come to realize that I am here to embody the Divine Feminine (*another name for our collective soul life or wave function, which is seen as feminine just like the left brain and logic (d-mode) is considered masculine*). I am here to allow my body to be a residence for Her. Caring for my body as a temple is cared for – with love, loyalty and deep respect – is an expression of my devotion to Her.

Beneath anger is hurt, or the threat of being hurt. The Feminine aspect of life – our Soul Life – has been hurt.

She has been denigrated, abused, belittled, rejected and denied. Our conduct toward Her, our attitude toward Her, determines the face She turns to us. Her face reflects our treatment of Her. Our North American culture has much restitution to make in relation to Her.

My calling is to relate to Her – listen and respond to Her. I am called to live in service to Her, to anchor my soul in this world through my deeds, my body, and my creative works. This is the outcome (so far) of a state *(wave function)* I entered while painting. I moved beyond my ego *(d-mode)* into energetic flow. I stepped out of Doing *(d-mode)* into Being *(wave function)*. My intention shifted from completing a project to allowing a process to unfold. Wow...was it valuable!

Years later, I like looking at my painting. I see sparks of light flying from the fires that dance on the surface of the water. Seen symbolically, the flames of anger blooming out of the unconscious produced particles of light, particles of consciousness. This integrative episode involving body, mind and soul has brought meaning and purpose to my daily life. I am grateful for all of it – the inflammation, the anger, the risk of painting, the healing, the understanding, the call. I consider myself blessed.

Note: explanations in parentheses are those of the author, Summer Bozohora.

Peggy, eased into the wave function by leaving her judgments and fears behind, and was able to release energy that had been lodged in her body. Her painting was not something she foresaw would happen. The end product really is irrelevant except as a symbol of her process. The end product is the material reality and manifestation of the wave function she engaged in. The process of Co-Creation was trusted and a new thing was created from a blank canvas, from nothing or no-thing.

To allow creativity its appropriate place in our lives and our culture, our education and our family relationships is to allow healing to happen at a profound level. The intimacy of creativity corresponds to the mystical experience itself. ...Afterward, we know we have tasted something worth remembering, something that will last. And often we have a special gift to bestow on others because of the journey we have undergone in our creative work. (Fox, 2002, 9)

In my life, I began with a background in Art Therapy and bridged my experience with spontaneous inner imagery and intuitive psychotherapy and medicine. I soon realized that what I was doing was engaging in what Matthew Fox (1990) describes as active meditation or non-directed prayer, as coined by Larry Dossey (1989).

The differences between active and passive meditation or prayer are listed in the following table that I have adapted from Matthew Fox (1990, p. 224).

Taken and adapted from Wrestling with the Prophets (Harper, 1990) by Matthew Fox

Passive/Directed Meditation/ Prayer/Awareness	Active/Non-Directed Meditation/Prayer/Awareness
Just sitting	Surrendering to experience
Concentrating & repeating (chant/mantra)	Letting go
Turning off	Opening up
Externally directed	Inner directed
Imagery is given	Imagery arises spontaneously
A way of detachment	A way of connecting
A way of emptying	A way of achieving depth

With directed prayer or passive meditation, the practitioner has a specific goal, image, or outcome in mind. Non-directed prayer, in contrast, uses none of these strategies. "In non-directed prayer, the practitioner does not attempt to tell the universe what to do" (Dossey, 1989, p. 58). Directing a specific outcome of a prayer or meditation is judgment and is a form of mental violence. Finding a place to start, setting an intention, or focussing on a present sensation, emotion or situation, is different from deciding ahead of time what the goal or outcome is to be.

To open up and let go, we learn to Trust. Trust is one of the key concepts in being able to access the wave function, and is the 'T' in the IN-OWT acronym.

I have an innate trust in the process and the Laws of Healing that have developed over time with years of experience. They allow me to connect quickly and drop into the wave function of my being and in doing so, I am present. I am not thinking about the past, not judging the present or analyzing the future. While coaching Peggy, I wasn't worried if I was a good teacher or coach or anxious about the product Peggy was creating. My d-mode was off. Peggy's d-mode was turned off too. She was not concerned about what colour to use or where to place it or if it would look good enough to put on her wall. She was immersed in the process and felt energy rush through her arm, into the brush and onto the canvas.

While learning to engage the wave function of their being, it is not unusual for people to pop in and out of d-mode. That is the purpose of a skilled coach in this process. As a mentor, the consistent wave function of my being creates a channel and space for clients to resonate with. Through presence, engaging the wave function in the here and now, and without judgment, my soul is open to universal energies. This is what 'holding space' for others is. Shutting off our d-modes, disengaging our personalities and immersing ourselves in the collective and collaborative universal field.

I have worked with many people in many situations and have seen such profound insights, connections and healing within people that I know, beyond a shadow of a doubt, that I can never predict any of it. My thinking mind is limited and I am always in awe and am deeply and profoundly grateful to be a witness to what occurs. I know that my d-mode faculties and my personality can never offer the profound healing and insight that inevitably occurs when we drop into our wave function. When d-mode is off, the psychological concept of 'projection' is not possible. Rather than a projector, we become a sacred mirror and a witness for others. The wave function allows us access to the intuitive, timeless and sacred art of co-creation by engaging the collective field.

All of us have the capacity to learn how to connect to universal consciousness and become Cosmic Artists because all of us are Light beings with the capacity for these two types of thinking: particle/d-mode or wave function. It's a matter of learning to use it.

The principles of IN-OWT, which simply describe the direction of energy from inside-to-outside or from soul-to-personality, allow us to disengage d-mode and stay present in the wave-function. Of course, once we have played in the Universal field by engaging wave function, there is a time to come back, take what we have learned and implement it. Then, it's our personality's turn to engage d-mode to effect change in our lives that reflect our soul's calling.

CHAPTER 6

Soul-Side Out

Through my story in Chapters 1 and 2, I alluded to my personal and professional experiences bringing me to an understanding of a healing process, and from those experiences, recognizing the laws that apply to that kind of healing. Much of the information will sound familiar from previous chapters, but here it is presented with purpose and for your better understanding of what those laws are and how they work.

The 10 Universal Laws or Principles of Healing from the INside-OWT

1. **We live in a Participatory Universe**. That means we are co-creators of everything we experience. Our inner world of feeling has a direct bearing on the outer world; all things are connected.

   Historically, inner images, intuitions, dreams, and perceptions have been discouraged, passed over as insignificant and, in a number of ways, treated with insensitive hostility or violence. Focusing on the outer world, on our thoughts instead of our feelings, and our bodies instead of our souls, on material reality over spirit, creates a belief in separation between ourselves and the greater forces of Nature and the Universal matrix. This separation incites fear and the idea that one must fight or struggle through life.

Understanding moves us from attempting to control through fear and violence to healing. With a different life view, recovering health and well-being is not about blame, nor is it about fear or fighting what we perceive to be outside of us. Healing is about response-ability and claiming our power as a co-creator. When you view your life as a co-creator, your life becomes full of interesting adventures wrought with exciting experiences and challenges that inevitably guide us to what I see as life's treasures: inner peace, personal power and a sense of the ultimate, and an undeniable interconnectedness of all things.

2. **The Soul is "Real."** The Soul is our personal connection to the Universal Field of Consciousness, i.e., Universe/God/Creator. As human beings evolve into multisensory humans, we learn to encompass the senses that come from within – the non-physical qualities of energy. It's of the utmost importance to understand that the pilot waves of awareness of our soul are what create material reality.

Being unable to interpret or understand the meaning of the soul's language, does not make it less important or real. What may seem illogical, unimportant, or even flaky to our d-mode is of greatest consequence to our health!

If we accept that our body, our clothing and the houses we live in are *real* because we can see them and can also accept that our emotions and body sensations – hunger and pain for example – are real because we can feel them, then it's not a big leap to understand that the energies – thoughts, beliefs, dreams and images – that prelude these emotional and body sensations are also real and of importance.

Conventionally, we've made the mistake of trying to understand the meaning of the soul's language logically and from d-mode perspective. This is ironic because, as a species, we are at a very immature state of evolution to think that our d-mode and physical things are 'it!' Within each of us, if we stop our busy lives and listen, our soul speaks to us via the wave function. It is within the soul, this inner Soul Space, that our individual potential blossoms and where energetic renewal takes place. It is from this perspective, that we can see new ideas and our life's potential.

3. **The Body, Mind and Soul are a trinity and a mutually defining and communicating system of light.** Through IN-OWT, one understands the soul to be one's connection to the universe and that the body, driven by the personality, is an instrument of the soul, all of which are systems of Light.

Light is energy and causes electric and magnetic fields. Photons of light travel through space with characteristics of both particles and waves. Physicists call this the wave-particle duality of light. The wave-particle duality of light means that everything in our world is either in its particle or wave state. From this theory it follows that our bodies are dense heavy forms of light in its particle state. Gary Zukav states, "Your personality is the energy of your soul converted to matter. ... Physical matter is the densest, or heaviest level of Light" (Zukav, 1989, p. 111 & 130).

Einstein, with great insight, realized that mass (i.e., matter) and energy are really different forms of the same thing. His famous equation ($E=MC^2$) is a mathematical statement that says that energy cannot be created nor destroyed, only transformed.

> *The* creation of physical experience through intention, the infusion of Light into form, energy into matter and soul into body, are all the same. The distance between you and your understanding of the creation of matter from energy is equal to the distance that exists between the awareness of your personality and the energy of your soul. ... The system is identical. (Zukav, 1989, p. 130)

Consciousness is not static; it flows into and out of matter, into waves and particles and back. If it is true that I am Light, I have the ability to engage either property of light – particle or wave. Candace B Pert, Former Chief of Brain Chemistry with the National Institute of Mental Health, suggests consciousness need not be centred in the brain.

> I can no longer make a strong distinction between the brain and the body.... The research findings indicate that we need to start thinking about how consciousness

can be projected into various parts of the body." (quoted by Larry Dossy) (Pert, 2018)

Likely because many people have been so focused on external cues perceived through the five senses, our internal senses have not been identified or distinguished. Instead, they have been lumped into one broad category referred to as the sixth sense. This sixth sense perceives vibrations or waves that are not visible to the eye. These vibrations and energies cannot be seen like material objects can be, but the feelings and e-motions they generate *are* felt physically, and have an impact on our physical well-being.

4. **We are Spiritual Beings having a Human Experience**. The intent of INside-OWT is to make the soul's needs known AND relay this information to the personality to carry out.

5. **The Soul is Time-Less**. The personality is that which encompasses the characteristics of a person – race, creed, gender, behaviours, and habits that one acquires over a lifetime. When one's physical body dies, these characteristics no longer exist; they are a function of historical context of that personality. The soul on the other hand is a timeless entity and its essence remains unchanged.

> Your personality is the part of you that was born into, lives within, and will die with, time. Your personality, like your body, is the vehicle of your evolution. … Every experience that you have upon the Earth encourages the alignment of your personality with your soul. *(Zukav, 1989, 29, p. 31)*

Without the spiritual act of recovering our soul, that immortal part of us that transcends space, time and personality, we will continue to act from isolation, fear and defensiveness, and will continue to attract adversity and inflict harm on nature and each other.

6. **We are Remembering a Time-Less Language.** In my experience, my soul wants to listen to the meaning imparted by a symptom or illness or situation in life. It is my judgmental mind (left brain or d-mode) that wants it to go away.

From the perception of the multisensory human, the physical world is a learning environment that is created jointly by the souls that share it, and everything that occurs within it serves their learning." (Zukav, 1989, p. 28)

The language of the soul is a function of the right brain and the wave function of Light. It encompasses internal senses such as emotion, feeling, inner images, inner sound and voices, physical sensations such as twinges, flutters, and pain – while awake or dreaming. Sufi Mystic Hazrat Inayat Khan calls the soul's language Cosmic Language (Khan, 1972). Jeanne Achterberg describes it as a preverbal or *a priori* language (Achterberg, 1995). *A priori* means a language that has always existed. It is a language we all possess when we are born, a language of archetypal images, symbols and feelings. It is a language that speaks of the deep interconnection and purpose of mankind.

7. **The Heart is the Physical Organ of the Soul.** The heart is the power-house or enlivening organ of the body. It is responsible for the maintenance of light energy in our body. Our hearts are at the core of the electrical and magnetic fields that communicate with the world around us. According to the scientists at the Institute of HeartMath:

> The electrical strength of the heart's signal, measured by an electrocardiogram (EKG), is up to 60 times as great as the electrical signal from the human brain, measured by an electroencephalogram (EEG), the heart's magnetic field is as much as 5,000 times stronger than that of the brain. ... When we form heart-centered beliefs within our bodies, ... we're creating the electrical and magnetic expression of them as waves of energy, which aren't confined to our hearts or limited by the physical barrier of our skin and bones. So clearly we're 'speaking' to the world around us in each moment of every day through a language that has no words: the belief-waves of our hearts. (Braden, 2008, p. 59-60)

Thus our inner light, our soul, is an energy field and its eminence is governed by our heart-based beliefs. Congruence between our thoughts (d-mode) and our hearts (wave function) heals dis-ease. The power of two interconnecting waves has been a symbol of medicine for centuries. The caduceus used as a symbol of medicine has two snakes wrapped in opposite directions on a staff or wand and is carried by two wings. It is the symbol of the power to move between realities, between the waking consciousness, personality or ego, that is bound by our material reality and our spiritual consciousness, or soul, that is unbounded by time and space. Our spiritual consciousness accesses the wave function and has the power to create and initiate change.

8. **Truth is a feeling of congruence and harmony between one's thoughts (d-mode/personality) and feelings (wave-function/soul).** It is easy to identify when we are not experiencing truth because we experience feelings that characterize fear; feelings such as anger, greed, resentment, revenge, and jealousy. "Feelings ... are the means through which we can discern the parts of itself that the soul seeks to heal, and through which we come to see the action of the soul in physical matter" (Zukav, 1989, p. 44).

   Negative or violent feelings are indicators that we need to further develop our relationship with our soul. Martin Buber, (Jewish philosopher) said: 'All suffering prepares the soul for vision.' But suffering is not necessary for vision if we are willing to look – to see – in the dreams and events of our lives, the all-important messages that are designed to bring us out of victim role and into victory. Most suffering is the result of not seeing. (Williston, 1995)

9. **Negative Energy is an Essential Part of our Being.** Negative is not 'bad'. Somehow in the development of human consciousness the natural poles of energy, negative and positive, have come to mean bad and good. The universe does not judge, human beings do.

The body is energized through the soul and is like a battery. Energy wants to stay in motion and batteries only work when there is a free-flow of energy from one pole (negative) to the other (positive). However, human beings in our current society and culture, have been taught to avoid or reject the negative and prefer, long for, or even obsess over the positive. We need negative energy, it is how we learn. Accepting, honouring, and trusting that it has something to teach you, is the only way for your energy to shift to the positive pole and retain your life-energy. Everything is energy – symptoms, situations, illnesses and dreams are all accompanied by e-motion (energy in motion) – keep it moving! and stop judging!

10. **Non-violence means non-judgment.** Judgment is violence. When we work with INside-OWT we must remember that we are not fixing something we perceive as wrong – rather we are serving something greater than ourselves and that we don't know all the answers. Ironically, happiness, health and well-being happen when you don't focus on trying to achieve them. "For success, like happiness, cannot be pursued; it must ensue and it only does so as the unintended side-effect of one's personal dedication to a cause greater than oneself" (Frankl, 1984, p. 17).

The Meaning of the Acronym IN-OWT and the Process of Healing

Immerse	Notice	Own	Willingness	Trust
yourself in your inner being	what comes up	what is presented	to play and accept the metaphorical processes	that you are safe & guided

The acronym of IN-OWT stands for: **I**mmerse. **N**otice. **O**wn. **W**illingness to play. **T**rust.

Immerse, **N**otice, **O**wn, **W**illingness to play, and **T**rust, are five key concepts in any healing process or journey. In a single session, a person may cycle through each of these steps several times, and not necessarily in order. This process takes us into learning how to trust our observations, our intuition and our own soul language, whether we are the person on the inward journey or the mentor who is the witness, or supporting guide.

While people cycle through their process and follow the energy trail, there are different signs that indicate people are reverting to d-mode or that they are experiencing a deep inner shift. There are various ways to mentor yourself or someone else so the journey stays focused, leading to insights and healing rather than just floating through and getting frustrated with random images and sensations.

I go through the indications and give suggestions of how you, as a mentor, might help yourself, or someone else get the most out of the process. I discuss these specific parts of the process and provide workbook pages to photocopy in the Companion Workbook, Section 7 of this book.

The principles and laws inherent in the process of INside-OWT short circuit the Symptom Imperative.

Remember, in Chapter 2, I talked about symptoms – either physical, emotional, or mental – being our friends. If you have ever had a good friend who wanted a heart-to-heart talk, you know no matter how nervous you are, in order to grow, you must be willing to sit down, in a quiet place, with an open heart, and *immerse* yourself in the moment. You must be able to look your friend (symptom) in the eye, hear what it has to say and *notice* your responses, looking for the truth in what they say and be willing to *own* that truth and take responsibility for it. It is also very useful to be *willing to play* and use humour to lighten the mood in any situation! Finally, you must *trust* the unfolding process will bring insight or resolution.

The Interpretation of the Acronym

 **To Immerse yourself,** set your intention to delve within your inner being and surrender to your soul. Sink in by finding a quiet place (within and without). Using breath as a way of making space within and focusing your attention on your heart (truth) centre in the middle of your chest. (See the workbook for a script and downloadable audio of this process)

This is a powerful, but not the only way to begin. You also can start by focusing on an image or word that seems to keep popping into your awareness, an emotional feeling, or a physical issue. Be aware of whatever holds or draws your attention. Nightmares and recurring dreams can be resolved with the same process – recalling part of a dream is enough to start.

 To Notice means paying attention to what is in your present awareness and *following the energy trail.* The energy trail may be a recent dream, or any images, internal sounds or words, sensations, memories, external distractions, or sounds that seem to draw your attention. Noticing is very difficult for many people. Most people tend to skip out and avoid noticing and go on to distract themselves with thoughts of such things as grocery lists or something else external.

As a person *follows the energy trail,* and is able to accept, honour, and trust what it presents, the energy moves throughout the body. It flows like an internal movie. Within the mind's eye, colours, strange images, body twinges, aches, and inner voices of wisdom can be sensed.

Thoughts that support and bring insight to these sensations are also part of the energy trail, while thoughts that are judgments are distractions. Aspects of oneself, often called our 'inner voice,' naturally emerge. People can and do name these personal aspects of themselves with various terms: inner child or child-self, one's mental or critical self, head or brain, one's guiding light or spirit, kernel or spark and many others. *(Personal terms derived from the client's own understanding occur spontaneously when needed and are preferred to those predetermined by psychological or medical definitions. The client's internal frame-of-reference is what determines healing.)*

As the movie unfolds within our mind's eye, the story of our identity unfolds. The meaning of each life experience can be witnessed and new truths and understandings integrated. The body feels the energetic shift through emotions and body sensations. In every case, when one approaches the feeling of fear and the unknown with courage and trust, as opposed to resistance or judgment, an insight, revelation, change in perspective or other surprising gift is inevitably received.

Owning your experience means accepting and acknowledging whatever the energy trail presents to you, despite how your logical mind wants to judge, avoid, or discount it. By staying with the energy trail, you show courage to move beyond what you previously thought possible. Some images appear scary and dark, but remember that darkness and evil simply represent the absence of light. As we accept, honour, and trust our inner world as a single benevolent force, by attuning our consciousness to the darkness within ourselves, we are shedding light on our shadow. "Once we reconcile the powers of light and darkness as elements of the same force, the question becomes: How do we use this unified force in our lives?" (Braden 2007, p. 129).

Willingness to play with the energy trail is very important. It means being open to suggestions, questions, and games, and not bound by rules of logic that we have been taught define the material world. During our immersion into our Soul-Self, it is natural for images and thoughts to emerge that do not necessarily make sense to our rational mind. Rest assured, images are metaphorical, not literal, which means they are NOT rational or linear.

As you start the process, it is helpful to know that your left-brain or conscious d-mode will tend to judge, avoid, and push away what seems unacceptable, weird, or scary. The key is to accept, honour, and trust whatever comes to you. At first it's like learning to drive in Australia (if you are from Canada or the U.S.) where the steering wheel is on the right side of the car and you drive on the left side of the road. It feels a little strange and the road signs can catch us off guard.

Trusting the energy trail is essential and is perhaps the hardest hurdle when a five-sensory personality starts to experiment with its new-found inner realm.

Five-sensory personalities could also be called spiritual agoraphobics, like their counterparts who suffer from the *psychological* affliction of agoraphobia – the fear of open places – *spiritual* agoraphobics have a deep seated fear of vast expanses; the infiniteness in time and space suggested by the nonlocal mind. They feel safer when things are closed in, finite, and 'local' – such as the mind that is confined to the individual brain and body, and a mind that stays put in the here and now. A mind in other words, that is soulless. (Dossey, 1989, p. 9)

Convincing the personality to hand its external power over is ultimately left to trust. There are no right, wrong or inappropriate answers. Your images simply tell you the truth about your belief systems and the feelings that need realignment. When you extend yourself, with the certainty that everything is okay even when you do not have proof, you recognize that you are safe.

CHAPTER 7

The INside-OWT Companion Workbook - Guidelines and Tools for Success

Definitions

Soul Searcher: The person who is setting the intention to explore their inner realms and the universal matrix of energy by accessing their wave function.

Mentor/Witness: The person who is offering to be the support, guide or witness to the soul searcher to help them stay present to the wave function. They assist the soul searcher in identifying when they have switched back into d-mode and help them re-engage and trust the process.

> **NOTE:** At times, the mentor and the soul searcher could be the same person. As skill develops, this process enables individuals to explore their own symptoms. This is a very empowering skill. There are some limitations to being a self-guided mentor, such as getting past some d-mode default settings we have. It's just easier for others to help us past our d-mode settings as an outside observer. I encourage both personal exploration (being the soul searcher and mentor to yourself) and switching roles

with others. As you practise, you increase your skill in the overall intuitive process. The practice deepens your knowledge of the unseen realms of the wave function and the universal matrix to which we belong. Over time, your personality adjusts to this new information and your life starts to look very different.

I have my own mentors to help me see. Many of them are the soul-searchers who grace me with their presence. Some think that if I have written this book I would not need mentorship. It couldn't be farther from the truth. I need more because I've written this book. In our western culture we have placed a high value on independence and I believe this comes at a great cost.

We live in a "mutually communicating (and defining) universe of meaning" (OMurchu, 2004). Without my interaction and realignment each day with the matrix and those with which I am able to construct meaning out of from our mutual desires and growth, I would be devastatingly unwell.

The Meaning of the Acronym IN-OWT and the Process of Healing

Immerse	Notice	Own	Willingness	Trust
yourself in your inner being	what comes up	what is presented	to play and accept the metaphorical processes	that you are safe & guided

The acronym of IN-OWT stands for: **Immerse. Notice. Own. W**illingness to play. **T**rust.

Immerse, **N**otice, **O**wn, **W**illingness to play, and **T**rust, are five key concepts in any healing process or journey. In a single session, a person may cycle through each of these steps several times, and not necessarily in order. This process takes us into learning how to trust our observations, our intuition and our own soul language, whether we are the person on the inward journey or the mentor who is the witness or supporting guide.

Remember in Chapter 2, I talked about symptoms (physical, emotional, or mental) being our friends. As we use the principles in the process of IN-OWT, we approach any aspect of ourselves – a difficult emotion, situation, illness, or symptom – like a friend, with quiet presence, openness and acceptance, honour and respect, we listen and observe. This is the case if we are the soul-searcher or the witness.

The process is such that you must be willing to sit down, in a quiet place, with an open heart, and *immerse* yourself in the moment. You must be able to look your friend (symptom) in the eye, hear what it has to say and *notice* your responses, looking for the truth in what they say and be willing to *own* that truth, to take responsibility for it. It is also very useful to be *willing to play* and use humour to lighten the mood. Finally, you must *trust* the unfolding process will bring insight or resolution.

Either as the soul-searcher or the mentor, it is a great honour to allow this process to take place and to be a witness to its unfolding.

What you may experience during IN-OWT sessions

These are some of the experiences clients have had during sessions or just after sessions.

- Understanding of emotional or physical symptoms and the spiritual lessons within them.

- A clear understanding of parts of yourself that have been hidden, neglected, wounded or repressed.

- An ability to observe and witness past events or memories without attachment, which allows the events to be released and healed energetically.

- Enhanced ability to dream, remember, and process dreams.

- The ability to trust your body, images, dreams, and symptoms as spiritual-life friends.

- An ability to look beyond the veils and false beliefs to trust the metaphorical and spiritual significance of your life.

- The ability to transcend the time-space reality and experience one-ness.

- A deep experience with your sense of the Creator, God, or the Universe.

- Appearance of Angels, Spirit Guides, or Animal Guides.

- An experience of past lives.

- An ability to connect with relatives who have passed on.

- A clear sense of spiritual direction or life purpose.

Immersion - A Suggestion for a Simple Beginning

It is useful to prepare a space with some ambient or brain wave music. I often use music from Chuck Wild and his series called Liquid Mind. My favourite title is *Slow World,* which helps soul searchers enter and stay in a theta brainwave state.

A Script for Immersion (Use a slow, soft voice)

Go to: www.body-mind-soul-coaching.com/immersion-audio-gift.html to download your FREE audio of how to get started. It will guide you in how to **Immerse** yourself into your inner being.

I invite you to set your own intention to take this time for yourself as you are now. Let the day's thoughts about what you need to do, or any worries or stressors, slip away for now; they will always be there for you to address later. I invite you to become aware of your surroundings, such as noises in the room, but we won't focus on them either. I'll invite you to be aware of your body sinking into the earth – Mother Nature's gravity-hug – allowing yourself to fall into that support. Now become aware of your breath and notice that it happens without you thinking about it. And from your heart centre (your truth) in the middle of your chest, I'll invite you to take a breath and become aware of a focus or intention for the session, whatever is in your present moment of awareness.

Staying on Track.

While people cycle through their process and *follow the energy trail,* there are different signs that indicate people are reverting to d-mode or that they are experiencing a deep inner shift. There are various ways to mentor yourself or someone else so the journey stays focused, leading to insights and healing rather than just floating through and getting frustrated with random images and sensations.

Unlike psychological work where one person is considered the expert – this work is done on a mutual and common playing field and in the universal field of the wave function. One person is the witness, the guide or conduit who holds the space, but the experience is recognized as mutually created, thus both the mentor and the soul searcher have responsibility for speaking their truth about what they are observing.

As a witness, you have the gift of sharing in the soul searcher's experience and it is important to be open to feel and experience what the client is feeling – to go with the energy and let it pass through you. In other words, as the witness you need to be able to stay centred or to continually redirect yourself to the wave function aspect of your being. As you build trust in the process, it becomes easier and easier to do and feeling gratitude for the transformations that take place increases the level of trust each time.

Naming Your Experience

In many psychological realms, there are professional terms derived and developed to help classify or explain different internal experiences or aspects of oneself: Inner Child, Inner Critic, etc. Although these terms can be useful, using terms that are not self-derived during the process of IN-OWT brings us back to d-mode.

During the process of IN-OWT, aspects of oneself, often called our inner voices, naturally emerge. People can and do name these personal aspects of themselves with various terms: inner child or child-self, one's mental or critical self, head or brain, one's guiding light or spirit, kernel or spark, and many others.

Personal terms derived from the client's own understanding (or the mentor's insights) occur spontaneously when needed and are preferred to those predetermined by psychological or medical definitions. This is because the client's internal frame of reference is what determines healing. If we use others' definitions or terms, we end up reverting to d-mode.

Staying in the Wave-Function.

It's fairly easy to identify when either the soul searcher or mentor has shifted into d-mode. The process stalls, there is an awkward silence, or the soul searcher cannot identify with the process when asked to describe their experience. They literally say they started thinking about their current stressors or their grocery list. As the mentor, it's important to know how to be a supportive guide (to others or oneself) and how to redirect the soul searcher back to the wave function when needed.

It is useful to remember that preconceived knowledge from any type of learning or schooling can interrupt and circumvent the transformational process because it is d-mode-generated and based on pre-established thought structures.

For example one of my colleagues Jessie, immersed herself in a INside-OWT session with me. Her intention and focus for the session was to be present and show up for herself. During the session, as she *immersed* herself, she instantly got a vivid black and white image of herself at the age of 10 years old curled up in a ball, feeling angry and on the edge of hysteria.

In her session, Jessie, verbally described her experience and said *"I tried* to pick her child-self up to rock and cradle her while sending her the message that she is enough," but she observed that her child-self became very stiff. At this point in the session, Jessie became confused as to why her child-self would be stiff at the suggestion that she is enough. The answer goes to the heart of what d-mode is. Telling oneself or a client that they are enough is a pre-existing answer, a static pre-formulated script that comes from d-mode and tells that person what they *should* think or how they *should* be; it's a judgment. It's not necessarily wrong to tell someone they are enough, but the route to actually feeling enough needs much more than a preconceived thought. A client needs to feel they are enough and that feeling can really only come from the undeniable truth at the centre of their soul that is accessible through the wave function state.

I have bolded the word ***tried*** in the above paragraph because it is an indicator that Jessie has jumped into using d-mode. Jessie became stuck in her process because sending the message she is enough is contrived. Anytime a soul searcher uses the word 'try' to describe how they are navigating their inner experience, it means they are in d-mode. In the wave function state everything flows, there is no need to force it by *trying*. This is what Jessie describes as her experience during this session:

> I moved into d-mode to speed up the process because I wanted the emotional discomfort to end. I wanted to reach the goal of resolution because I didn't want to tolerate the emotional pain or process anymore so I jumped to *thinking* of a solution (d-mode). I tried to do this by using a technique I had experienced in a psychodrama session at an earlier time in my life, which was to meet the unmet need the child within me was feeling. In the context of the psychodrama session this was what I needed. However, it was ***not*** what I needed during our INsideOWT session. I was trying to force an old solution onto a new problem.

From a previous experience, Jessie learned to send the message to her child-self that she is enough. Although the intention seems good, it is still a method of force or fixing and the result (the child being stiff and Jessie being confused) is a clear indication that Jessie is not being present, not trusting, and is subtly attempting to force the child to feel something she does not.

Because Jessie was stalled in her process, as a mentor, I made the suggestion and redirected her back to the wave function with this statement: "Check in and see how she feels." Jessie's immediate response was "OH!.. She's stiff! She needs to move. She really likes her shawl and to have it on her body…" and the session progressed from there.

What I would like to emphasize here, is that as human beings, we all do this. We all try to make situations fit a certain mold or belief structure we have been brought up with or professionally trained in without realizing we do it.

Making situations fit molds or belief structures is d-mode. D-mode is great for logical problem solving in existing structures, like how to change a muffler on a car. However, when we want to change a feeling state or perception of reality from an existing emotional wound, we can't treat it like a mechanical d-mode problem. The wave function must be engaged and we must be willing to enter a mutually shared reality in the Universal matrix.

In the situation and story I just shared, Jessie was in the role of the soul-searcher and I was gifted as her witness to share in the learning of the IN-OWT session. However, the soul searcher in me gained a great deal of energetic knowledge as to how damaging this d-mode behaviour actually is when we apply it to the wrong types of problems.

This particular example also teaches us that we can only deeply be of service as a mentor or witness if we can also be moved as a mutual soul searcher feeling the significance of the session on a universal level. In this example, as a mentor, we must be able and willing to *feel* the position of the child being told to feel like she is enough. If I was not engaged in the wave-function, if I was wearing a hat of a counsellor and slipped into my d-mode training, I would likely have been just as confused because it seemed the logical and 'right' thing to do to tell the child she is enough.

That is the gift of the wave function state. Images within the matrix tell us the truth through feeling and precise metaphor. By the end of the session, Jessie's 10-year-old child was dancing (as opposed to stiff) and in full colour (as opposed the black and white image at the beginning), a clear indicator of a transformative shift in the state of Jessie's inner 10-year-old.

Guidelines for INside-OWT Work

Notice and take response-ability for what you are learning. In the co-creative work of INside-OWT, you are literally co-creating your experience. The amount of dialogue that goes on between the soul searcher and mentor depends on the skill of each person. In the beginning there may be quite a bit of dialogue. As the mentor and soul searcher increase their skill and confidence, less verbal dialogue takes place.

<u>Responsibility of the Soul Searcher</u>

It is your responsibility to aid your mentor and let them know what helps you or hinders you in your process. Notice if you feel uncomfortable with sharing what you need. It means it is an important growth area for being able to express your truth.

Experiments and suggestions of the mentor can be modified or completely ignored if they do not serve you or deepen your experience. After each session, you will note and track yourself, as to what stage in the process you are able to get to and whether or not you came full circle. Be honest, it will help you find starting points for other sessions. Track yourself and watch for repetitive images.

<u>Responsibility of the Mentor or Witness</u>

TAKE NOTES: Write down the soul searcher's initial intention and whatever they say during their process. After they are done with their own process of journaling they may appreciate you reading back your notes so they can write down anything that is important to them.

As a witness and a co-creator of the process, accept, honour, and trust your own feelings. Be honest, if you are uncomfortable with the soul searcher's images and find it difficult, start to judge, try to help or fix, or you are being 'triggered' acknowledge your truth. Your acknowledgment is a great gift in the process. It is a teacher of present moment awareness and truth and your acknowledgment builds trust.

The type of support you offer is very important. The session is not about your logical understanding. We are not interrogating or probing; we are supporting another to fully experience their inner world. When we offer support by way of questions, it is important the intention is either to a) clarify what you heard the soul searcher say, or b) to deepen their inner experience by posing questions in and around the metaphor they are experiencing. We don't need to understand it, fix it, or change it.

Encouragement and Support from the Mentor

During the course of the INside-OWT session, the mentor has a few options and ways of supporting the soul searcher. I often use comments such as:

- "What are you noticing now?"
- "Good awareness."

Above all, be sure to laugh with and cry with the soul searcher. Feel. The process is a wonderful journey into the breadth and fullness of being alive.

Questions, Experiments and Suggestions Made by the Mentor

Questions, experiments or suggestions made by the mentor are to help deepen the soul searcher's internal exploration and should relate to the metaphor, image, or sensation the soul searcher is experiencing.

- "Can I make the suggestion of …" or

- "I have an idea for an experiment."

For example, if the soul searcher is experiencing 'spinning'… and can't seem to stop, ask them about the spinning. A natural question might be: What direction are you spinning? How fast? Sideways? Up? Down?, etc. Although the sensation may be uncomfortable, remember that the premise of IN-OWT is to stay in the wave function, watching the sensations shift and change as we accept, honour, and trust our inner world. Our inner world of the wave function and its images is not bound by the same rules as d-mode. We must hold faith and an open space for transformation when the intensity and fear builds in the soul searcher, who may want to exit the experience and default back to the perceived safety and control of d-mode.

How to Identify when the Soul Searcher has slipped into d-mode

Key d-mode words to watch for:

I **"Think" "Try"** or **"Trying"** to **"Do"** something

In the example of the sensation of spinning, the soul searcher may say "I am *trying* to stop the spinning." Then the mentor has the opportunity to redirect the soul searcher to further understanding and integration of the image or sensation by using or modifying one of these suggested statements:

- I notice you are thinking because I heard you say…

- I notice you are really trying to do X (*stop the spinning*), are you able to let go of trying and see what happens? Just be curious, notice and watch

- Repeat back key words or feelings

- Invite them to feel X (*spinning*) more fully

- What do you notice? or What are you aware of now?

- Encourage play by being playful yourself

- What does X (*the spinning*) remind you of?

- Remind them: in a journey anything can happen

- Remind them that they can ask questions of the images

- Remember to accept, honour, and trust

- Keep breathing. As you breathe into what your body is presenting, it is able to keep moving

- Share any intuitive insight that you have

- Share what you see or feel happening in the image.

Watch for NON-VERBAL Cues

The soul searcher gives clues about their states that will help you discern how to best support them.

- Facial Expression

- Tears

- Body twitches or holding

- Breath – watch for erratic or shallow breath

- Deep Integration Breath.

When a soul searcher is in d-mode, people often hold their breath and their facial expressions will appear strained or confused. When soul searchers are in their wave function state, there is an energy of peace, acceptance, tears of joy or often amazement. At times there will be involuntary body twitches and soul searchers will take deep belly breaths at the point of an integration or awareness.

As a mentor, you don't have to be perfect, just yourself. It is a great opportunity as a witness to test your perceptions and intuition and how you receive them. The focus is on the journey of the soul searcher, but as a guide and co-creator, it may be important to share what you feel and see as you engage the wave function with the soul searcher.

Coming Full Circle – Finding resolution

An INside-OWT journey is complete or has come *full circle* when there is a resolution to the pinnacle, conflict, fear, or struggle that occurred. Remember to *check back* to the original intention or other important aspects or images within the journey. For example, if the first focus was a body ache or pain, have the soul searcher check in with that – is it as strong or completely gone? If the original intention was an image, see if the image has shifted or changed. This will give you a clue as to the level of resolution that has occurred.

Journalling and Application

It is often helpful for soul searchers to write down and impart the wave function information to the personality to carry out. It can be helpful, but not necessary for the mentor to read back any notes taken during the session. How this part of the session takes place is very individual. A verbal debriefing can take place between mentor and Soul searcher about how the personality can apply the souls information.

More importantly than how – whether its processed in silence, in written or verbal form – after each soul session a time of integration is needed whereby the energy can sift through the mind and body into the awareness of the personality to carry out. I strongly encourage soul searchers either to take an entire sabbatical from work for several months, or if not that, at least the day off work when a session is in progress.

Without the application of and action taken on part of the personality from the information imparted during the soul session, we may as well play video games and watch the images in amusement for periods of brief distraction from what we believe our life to be.

After the sessions and the integration of the journeys, the practice comes in displaying courage and discipline to change our lives with the new knowledge. Sometimes change is immediate and astonishing, at other times, with more ingrained patterns, it can take patience and persistence. The emergence of wave function knowledge into the slower and denser world of material things, is imminent, but not always instant. Having patience and meeting with doubt or other types of resistance is another area where trust comes into play and where the practice of applying the five steps of IN-OWT over and over can help us reinforce the knowledge and make the changes we desire.

Hints for Processing Physical Symptoms

Health is commonly defined in our culture as the absence of symptoms or the elimination or control of disease. Healing moves us from attempting to cure or control through war and fear (conquering disease and fighting infection) to understanding.

The mental thoughts and feelings that precipitate the most disease in the body are criticism, anger, resentment, guilt, shame, grief, and fear. Being able to energetically forgive, let go, and redirect anger into a form that enables you to stand up for yourself and create healthy boundaries in relation to others (changing your perception of yourself and your world, both inner and outer) is much of the healing work.

The deep understanding of a symptom's meaning is most easily accessed when the symptoms are obvious or aggravated, i.e., when the energy behind physical symptoms are readily present, because the self-defense mechanisms of the ego or child-self are lowered and open to transformation. Symptoms 'talk' both through physical symptoms, but also through feeling, sound and metaphor in images, dreams, and symbols. Even though we may lack understanding or ignore these messages, they will stay ever present in us until we heed or begin to hear or see their messages. Symptoms are persistent friends. They always stay with you no matter how badly you judge them, avoid them, or ignore them. They want to be loved and they want the message and meaning of what they are imparting to you to be re-integrated, so you can be a more soul-filled, heart-centered being.

There are several 'helpful hints' that apply to seeking the meaning of symptoms. Taken and adapted from the book, *The Body's Messages,* by Michael J. Lincoln, PhD.

1. First, it is better not to focus the physical mechanics of the symptoms. This is because physical mechanics take us into analyzing the symptom with our rational left-brain and d-mode that cannot make the deep connections required for healing. This is also because it is not the real basis of the problem. It is fine to acknowledge, and sometimes helpful to understand, the body's process, but it is far more helpful if we engage this knowledge in a symbolic and metaphorical way, rather than a causal one.

2. Second, it is helpful to work out the exact point in time when each symptom appeared. Look into the life situation, along with the thoughts, feelings, fantasies, dreams, events, and issues that were operating at the time. It also helps to look into the preceding period that led up to larger events. The events that precipitated the major illnesses or accidents can usually be found to have gotten to a critical point 6-12 months prior.

3. Third, it is useful to pay attention to the language that is reflective and symbolic of what is being manifested. For example idioms we use have deep significance, such as something "is getting under my skin" or, "I feel stuck between a rock and a hard place," or, "I can't keep my head above water," etc.

4. Fourth, asking what the symptom stops you from doing and what it has you doing that you would rather not leads directly to the illnesses central theme. For example, when someone develops a cold or flu it prevents them from going to work (which a person would rather not) and it allows a person to stop and rest and lay on a couch without guilt.

5. To really be able to access the symbolic and metaphorical meaning there are various resources that may help trigger your Aha if you know which body part is affected. Louise Hay has many books that are useful and you can research myths or body postures in Hatha yoga to help define and get a body-felt sense of the situation.

6. Relaxation is key. Using relaxing music, candles, the bath, or Yoga, or other gentle exercising, is excellent. Bodywork such as the Rosen Method, Myofacial Release, Craniosacral Therapy, and Chi Nei Tsang, also get the body's energy ignited for ease in accessing image-energy.

7. Breathe. Breath is key to allow the meaning to be imparted. Deep belly breathing makes space and circulates blood and oxygen flow throughout the body to initiate the parasympathetic nervous system, wherein healing takes place.

EXAMPLE:

I had been aware of my tight jaw for some time, but after the second body-worker I went to mentioned it, I chose to process the message it was giving me. One morning as I lay in bed half awake, I breathed into my tight jaw and explored the physical sensations, as I remained open to the experience, I was presented with an image of my upper and lower gums and teeth stuck together with some kind of gummy sticky glue. I could see in my mind's eye that it was red in colour and how it squished together when I tried to move my jaw.

To process my image I could have remained in my mind's eye, lying down in my soft mental state, but chose to sketch it out on paper instead. The resulting image turned out to look more like my jaw was on fire. While I drew, the word RESIDUE came to mind and still in a soft mental state I considered why my drawing looked more like fire than the original glue-like substance and my AHA came to me. The residue was red, hot, anger and resentment I had toward my husband when our daughter was born two years prior. I felt abandoned at the time and had been angrily observing and nit-picking his every house-cleaning habit since. When I recognized the reason for my negative behaviour and feelings, I was able to recognize them as feelings from the past that I was dragging into the present. With the recognition came a feeling of relief and I decided to stop nit-picking. Almost as soon as I made the decision, my husband began to participate freely in our household chores.

Following the Energy Trail: IN-OWT Tracking Sheet

Immersion is setting your intention to immerse yourself within your inner being.

MY INTENTION or Focus was:_____

Q: How easy was it to immerse yourself into your being this time?

NOTES:

_____

_____

Notice what is in your present awareness and 'follow the energy trail.' WHAT was in your energy trail? What images or themes emerged?

NOTES:

_____

_____

Own it. This means to accept and acknowledge whatever the energy trail presents, despite how our logical mind wants to dismiss, judge, avoid, or discount it. How is it for you to 'watch your internal movie... What do you notice about yourself? Is there anything you find difficult to accept or acknowledge?

NOTES:

_____

_____

Willingness to Play. The 'energy trail' is open to questions and games. It is not bound by rules of logic.

NOTES: Was there anything surprising that occurred?

NOTES: What things did your mentor do that were helpful to illicit play, i.e., what experiments did he or she offer? What was not helpful?

Trust. There are no right, wrong or inappropriate answers. When we trust our inner guidance system, an interior struggle, repulsive image, or painful feeling becomes a gift of awareness via a surprising shift of thought or change in feeling. In IN-OWT, this shift is called Full-Circle. Trust is perhaps the most important and perhaps the biggest obstacle when a person practises IN-OWT. Part of trusting is accepting what 'stage' of meditation you are able to achieve. The process is about progress, not perfection. IN-OWT is about listening to oneself, about the progression of being willing to hear and respond to one's inner truth. By accepting and honouring your truth in the moment, transformation occurs. **If you want to be anything or be anywhere other than where you are in life, including wishing you could have come full circle, you will continue to go in circles, instead!

NOTES: What else did I notice about myself during this process

---

REFERENCES

Achterberg, Jeanne. *(1985) Imagery in Healing: Shamanism and Modern Medicine.* Boston: Shambhala.

Berne, Samuel. (1994) *Creating your Personal Vision: A Mind-Body Guide for Better Eyesight.* Santa Fe, New Mexico: Color Stone Press.

Bly, Robert. (1975) *A Little Book on the Human Shadow.* New York: Harper Collins.

Bodenhamer, Bob. (2010) The Stress Fight/Flight/Freeze Pattern. Retrieved from http://www.neurosemantics.com/Stuttering/stress_pattern.html (accessed October, 2008)

Braden, Gregg. (2008) *The Spontaneous Healing of Belief: Shattering the Paradigm of False Limits.* New York: Hay House Inc.

Bradshaw, John. (1990) *Coming Home: Reclaiming and Championing Your Inner Child.* New York: Bantam.

—. (2001) *The Creative Life: 7 Keys to Your Inner Genius.* New York: Jeremy P. Tarcher/Putnam.

Cappachione, Lucia. (2001) *The Power of the Other Hand: A Course in Channeling the Inner Wisdom of the Right Brain.* New Page Books.

Clarke, Jean Illsley & Dawson, Connie. (1998) *Growing Up Again: Parenting Ourselves, Parenting our Children.* 2 ed. Minnesota: Hazelden.

Claxton, Guy. (1997) *Hare Brain, Tortoise Mind: How Intelligence Increases When You Think Less.* Great Britain: The Ecco Press.

Deepak, Chopra, MD. (1989) *Quantum Healing; Exploring the Frontiers of Mind/Body Medicine.* New York: Bantam Books.

Dispenza, Joe, MD. (2014) *You are the Placebo Effect – Making Your Mind Matter.* California: Hay House Inc.

Dossey, Larry, MD. (1989) *Recovering the Soul: A Scientific and Spiritual Search.* New York: Bantam Books.

—. (1993) *Healing Words: The Power of Prayer and the Practice of Medicine.* New York: Harper Paperbacks.

Fancher, Robert. (1995) *Cultures of Healing: Correcting the Image of American Mental Health Care.* New York: W.H. Freeman and Company.

Forfar, D.O. (1995) James Clerk Maxwell: Maker of Waves. James Clerk Maxwell Foundation. http://www.clerkmaxwellfoundation.org/Maker_of_Waves.pdf (accessed April, 2009).

Fox, Matthew. (1990) *Wrestling with the Prophets.* San Francisco: HarperSanFrancisco, a division of Harper Collins.

—. (1991) *Creation Spirituality: Liberating Gifts for the People of the Earth.* New York: Harper Collins.

—. (2002) *Creativity: Where the Divine and Human Meet.* New York: Putnam._

Frankl, Victor, E. (1984) *Man's Search for Meaning.* New York: Pocket Books.

Friedman, Norman. (1997) *The Hidden Domain Home of the Quantum Wave Function, Natures Creative Source.* Eugene, Oregon: The Woodbridge Group

Ganim, Barbara. (1999) *Art and Healing: Using Expressive Art to Heal Your Body, Mind and Spirit.* New York: Three Rivers Press.

Gardner, Howard. (2006) *Five Minds for the Future.* Boston: Harvard Business School Publishing.

Gold, Aviva. (1998) *Painting from the Source. Awakening the Artist's Soul in Everyone.* New York: Harper Perennial.

Goswami, Amit. (1999) *Quantum Creativity: Waking Up to Our Creative Potential.* New Jersey: Hampton Press Inc.

Grossman, Marc. (1998) *To Be Healed by the Earth*. Toronto: Hushion House.

Hawkins, David R., M.D. (2009) *Healing and Recovery.* Sedona: Veritas Publishing.

James Clerk Maxwell Foundation. *Who was James Clerk Maxwell?* Retrieved from http://www.clerkmaxwellfoundation.org/index.html (accessed April, 2009)

Jung, Carl G. (1964) *Man and His Symbols.* New York: Dell Publishing Group.

Jung, Carl G. (1971) Ed., Joseph Campbell. *The Portable Jung.* New York: Penguin.

Katie, Byron. (2002) *Loving What Is: Four Questions That Can Change Your Life*. New York: Harmony Books.

Khalsa, Narayan Singh. (1991) *Illnesses and Ailments: Their Psychological Meaning*. Cited in preface to *Messages from the Body*, by Michael J. Lincoln.

Khan, Hazrat Inayat. (1988) *Spiritual Dimensions of Psychology.* New York: Omega Publications.

Khan, Hazrat Inayat. (1972) *Cosmic Language.* Tucson, Arizona: Omen Press

Kopp, Richard R. (1995) *Metaphor Therapy.* New York: Brunner/ Mazell.

Kurtz, Ron. (1990) *Body-Centered Psychotherapy – The Hakomi Method.* Mendocino, California: Life Rhythm.

LeDoux, Joseph. (1996). *The Emotional Brain: The Mysterious Underpinnings of Emotional Life.* New York: Simon & Schuster Paperbacks.

Lipton, Bruce H., PhD. (2004) "Mind over genes-The new biology," *Alternatives Magazine*, No. 28, Retrieved from http://www.alternativesmagazine.com/28/lipton.html (accessed November 2008)

—. (2005) *Biology of Belief: Unleashing the Power of Consciousness, Matter and Miracles.* U.K.: Hay House.

Lusseyran, Jacques. (1963) *And There Was Light: Autobiography of Jacques Lusseryan, Blind Hero of the French Resistance.* New York: Parabola Books.

McNiff, Shaun. (1998a) *Art Based Research.* Philadelphia: Jessica Kingsley Publishers.

—. (1998b) *Trust the Process: An Artist's Guide to Letting Go.* Boston: Shambhala.

Millman, Dan. (1993) *The Life You Were Born to Live: A Guide to Finding Your Life Purpose.* Tiburon, California: H.J. Kramer Inc.

Mindell, Arnold. (2004) *The Quantum Mind and Healing.* Charlottesville, Virginia: Hampton Roads.

Muller, Wayne. (1999) *Sabbath – Finding Rest, Renewal and Delight in our Busy Lives.* New York: Bantam Books.

Nelson, Bradley. (2013) *The Emotion Code.* E-motion. Retrieved from Gaia.com

Newton's Dark Secrets. (2003) Produced for the BBC and WGBH Boston. DVD.

O'Murchu, Diarmuid. (2004) *Quantum Theology: Spiritual Implications of the New Physics.* New York: The Crossroad Publishing Company.

Oyle, Irving, MD. (1976) *Time, Space and the Mind: The mind's ability to switch off the time-space reality is the single, most powerful healing tool available to humanity.* Berkeley California: Celestial Arts.

Pert, Candace. (2018) Retrieved from https://oneandallwisdom. com/healing-quotations/

Remen, Rachel Naomi. (1994) The recovery of the sacred: Some thoughts on medical reform. *In Context:Good Medicine 39,* (Fall). Retrieved from http://www.context.org/ICLIB/IC39/Remen.htm (accessed September 2008).

—. (1996) In the Service of Life. *Noetic Sciences Review.* Spring.

Rosenberg, Marshall, PhD. (2005) *Speak Peace in a World of Conflict, What You Say Next Will Change Your World.* California: Puddle Dancer Press.

Rosenberg, Marshall. (2003a) *Nonviolent Communication: A Language of Life.* 2ed. Encinitas, California: Puddle Dancer Press.

—. (2003b) *Spiritual basis of nonviolent communication.* The Center for Nonviolent Communication. Retrieved from http://www.cnvc.org/en/what-nvc/spiritual-basis/spiritual-basis-nonviolent-communication (accessed December 3, 2009)

Sarno, John E., MD. (1991) *Healing Back Pain: The Mind-Body Connection.* New York: Warner Books.

Sarno, John E., MD. (2007) *The Divided Mind: Epidemic of Mindbody Disorders.* New York: Harper Collins.

Shlain, Leonard M. (2007) *Art & Physics.* New York: Harper Perennial.

Tiller, William A., Walter E. Dibble, and Michael J. Kohane. (2001) *Conscious Acts of Creation: The Emergence of a New Physics.* California: Pavior Publishing.

Tolle, Eckhart. (1997) *The Power of Now: A Guide to Spiritual Enlightenment.* Vancouver, British Columbia: Namaste Publishing Inc.

Weissman, Darren. (2013) *The Lifeline Technique.* Emotion. Retrieved from Gaia.com

Williamson, Marianne. (1992) *A Return To Love: Reflections on the Principles of a Course in Miracles.* New York: Harper Collins.

Zander, Rosamund & Zander, Benjamin. (2000) *The Art of Possibility: Transforming Professional and Personal Life.* Boston, Massachusetts: Harvard Business School Press.

Zukav, Gary. (1989) *The Seat of the Soul.* New York: Simon & Schuster Inc.

Contributors Contact Information

Summer Bozohora

Whole Body-Mind-Soul Coach
www.body-mind-soul-coaching.com
www.summerbozohora.com
Summer@summerbozohora.com

Michelle Enns

Intuitive & Spiritual Energy Healer
Live in the Light
Liveinthelight@michelleenns.com

Jill Sodero

Intuitive Counsellor & Spiritual Mentor
Discover Your Healing
www.jillsodero.com
info@jillsodero.com

Olivia Kachman

Phoenix Alchemy
www.phoenixalchemy.net
info@phoenixalchemy.net

Peggy Funk Voth

Jungian Analyst
www.peggyvoth.com
peggy@peggyvoth.com

Linda M. Verde

Book Editor and Writer
www.copywriteedit.ca
lindav287@gmail.com

CPSIA information can be obtained
at www.ICGtesting.com
Printed in the USA
BVHW030526310821
615483BV00001B/13